THE THEORY OF ARCHETYPES

The Theory of Archetypes

James S. Larson

Nova Science Publishers, Inc.
New York

Library of Congress Cataloging-in-Publication Data

The theory of archetypes / James S. Larson.
p. cm.
Includes index.
ISBN: 1-59454-062-4 (hardcover)
1. Archetype (Psychology) I. Larson, James S.

BF175.5.A72T48 2006
302'.1—dc22

2004008864

400 Oser Ave, Suite 1600
Hauppauge, New York 11788-3619
Tele. 631-231-7269 Fax 631-231-8175
e-mail: Novascience@earthlink.net
Web Site: http://www.novapublishers.com

Printed in the United States of America

To My Wife, Krista

CONTENTS

PREFACE

On Valentine's Day, 2002, I took my wife to a movie called *A Beautiful Mind*. In that movie, John Nash accused his fellow graduate students at Princeton of not having an original thought in their publications. As an academic, I felt convicted of not being original in my own research. Being a Christian, I prayed that God would give me something original to write about. He answered that prayer with the theory of archetypes.

Previously, I had done research on the conceptualization of health and was struck by the absence of spiritual health in modern definitions. It seemed obvious that man had a spiritual side, and that some were spiritually healthy while others were not. Health traditionally had been conceptualized as consisting of mind, body and spirit. Later, after some preliminary research, I found that Plato had proposed a linkage between mind, body and spirit and the three functions of government. Obviously, this was encouraging and lent credibility to my theory.

I would like to thank my wife, Krista, for her encouragement in the process of writing this book. I also would like to thank Renea Thompson and Shayne Watts for their research assistance in the chapters on sociology and anthropology.

I apologize to the reader for the use of extensive quotes in this book, but the breadth of the topic required this technique. Most scholars are not trained extensively in all of the social sciences, usually in just one or two of them. So, I found myself learning a great deal in the areas of sociology and anthropology. My doctoral degree is in political science, and I took extensive course work in economics as an undergraduate. I have always had an interest in psychology, and am self-educated in that field.

It is hoped that this new theory of archetypes will have broad application in the social sciences. If it does, it may contribute to the development of new theories within each discipline, theories that may be tested scientifically.

Ultimately, the hope is that these theories will produce testable hypotheses that can advance the state of knowledge in all of these disciplines.

J. Larson

> We know the truth not only through our reason but also through our heart. It is through the latter that we know first principles...
> ***Pascal, Pensees,***
> ***"Causes and effects"***

A PERSONAL INTRODUCTION

Charles T. Goodsell
Emeritus Professor of Public Administration
Virginia Tech

'This book presents an explicit theory of social science. It has long been my belief that the content of social theory reflects, to a substantial degree, the personal attitudes and worldviews of social theorists. Just as novelists, poets, and composers present their own personalities in their works, social theorists construct models, frameworks and paradigms that express not just the best possible "science" but their own personal attitudes and emotional orientations.'

This book gave me an opportunity to test my thesis. On the one hand, I had had the opportunity to read the manuscript twice without the author attempting to interpret it for me. Since I had had nothing to do with its development, I could look at it with some perspective. On the other hand, a quarter century ago the author was my doctoral student and wrote his dissertation under my direction. Hence I knew him quite well, although in later years we had had only infrequent contact. Thus, by knowing the theorist and seeing the theory, I was in a position to hold one up against the other. Did they "match" or not?

'As often happens in genuine empirical tests, the results are mixed. Part of the book I could have anticipated, but part is a surprise. As for the unsurprising aspects, I always found Jim to be a straight-forward, honest, and sincere individual. The present narrative possesses the same tone. The argument of the book is presented clearly, up-front, without a trace of cunning or artifice. Just to make sure you get them, all key points are summarized at the end of each chapter.

Also, although as a young man Jim never discussed his religious beliefs with me, his easy warmth and gentle manner suggested a sensitive, spiritual person. And how does the book begin?—with something rare in secular intellectual writings, an outright declaration of Christian faith.

Finally, I recall that Jim always showed a certain impatience as a student—a desire to move ahead quickly, do something out of the ordinary, and try different things in a new way. These qualities are, indeed, abundantly manifest in this volume. His ideas are incredibly bold, innovative, and creative. In fact, *The Theory of Archetypes* does nothing less than offer to its readers an elegant original theory of human nature and human knowledge.

'What is there about the book that I could not have anticipated? Three things. First, it is an exciting read. Jim's dissertation, previous books and numerous published articles, while solid, well researched, and useful contributions to their subjects, were not particularly provocative. This book, by contrast, is highly so. The coherence, drive, and momentum of the argument, which is that human understanding of the social world derives specifically from understanding of the self, is nothing short of remarkable. I recall that after my first read I could think of little else the rest of that day.

'Second, the book departs radically from Jim's previous work. His three earlier books and scores of published articles concern such practical matters as quantitative measures of health, health insurance policy, and failures of policy implementation. The closest his prior scholarship came to this theoretical realm was his concern for mental health and social well-being. One of the uses Jim gives for his archetypal framework is that it can aide in the diagnosis of social ills.

Third, the book is unusually synoptic. Jim surveys principal theories of politics, economics, psychology, sociology, and anthropology. He contends that common among them is a triad of elements that parallel the basic human archetypes of mind, body, and spirit. In government, for example, these correspond respectively to the legislative branch, executive branch, and judiciary. In Freudian psychology the parallels are ego, id, and super ego. In micro-economics, they are prices, wages, and taxes. Within all these triads, Jim believes, the same ideal patterns apply: balance (co-importance of the three), restraint (absence of excessive control by any), and priority (i.e., 1. Spirit, 2. Mind, and 3. Body).

'I leave it to the reader to form his or her own conclusions as to whether the analysis makes sense. But beyond doubt, in my mind, the book represents a well-crafted and exciting exercise in theoretical synthesis and boldness. True, when Jim was a graduate student, I could not have predicted that he would write this book someday. But, isn't that true for all of us? We human beings often have a potential for creativity within us that is securely hidden from view until it bursts forth. And, on those occasions, the rest of us can be stimulated.'

Chapter 1

MIND, BODY AND SPIRIT

As an undergraduate at Colgate, I remember a comment by a professor of foreign policy that has stayed with me. He remarked that one of his students had criticized his manner of lecturing, in which he grouped supporting arguments "in threes." He joked that he would try to come up with some twos and fours in the future.

The human mind seems attracted to organizing phenomena into groups of three. The game of twenty questions often begins with the question: "Is it animal, vegetable or mineral?" We organize our days around morning, afternoon and evening. The world around us is perceived as land, air and sea; or as earth, wind and fire. And biology recognizes three kingdoms of nature as plant, fungus and animal.

Famous theories and philosophies also are based on groupings of three. In philosophy, three types of reasoning are induction, deduction and analogy. The essence of Hegel's philosophy of history is thesis, antithesis and synthesis. Freud's describes man's psyche as id, ego and superego. And, Jefferson describes the fundamental rights of man as life, liberty and the pursuit of happiness.

The classification into threes also extends beyond human learning and appears in nature itself, suggesting that there is a design in nature. All matter is composed of solid, liquid or gas. The water cycle on earth consists of evaporation, condensation and precipitation. Primary colors in the spectrum of light are red, blue and yellow. And atoms are composed of protons, neutrons and electrons.[1]

In the field of cultural anthropology, Alan Dundes' essay "The number three in American culture" notes its importance to our culture. Dundes writes that one can "pick up an elementary textbook in any discipline and find numerous instances of three-determined thinking."[2] In fact, more recent scholarship "has demonstrated the existence of the pattern in most of Western civilization and has suggested it may be characteristic of Indo-European culture."[3]

MIND, BODY AND SPIRIT

One of the most fundamental ways that man views himself is in terms of mind, body and spirit. Before recorded history, man was aware of these three elements in himself and their interplay in his life. The awareness of body must have been almost instantaneous when pain, illness and strength became evident, as well as the various parts of the body. The awareness of mind must have been slower in coming, as man became aware of how the body was controlled, how thought directed its actions and how others seemed to be directed by different thoughts.

The awareness of spirit was more complex, as man became aware of forces in the natural world. The development of primitive art found in caves is "closely connected with a belief in magic."[4] Primitive people believed that other creatures and objects "were endowed with spirits like themselves."[5] Hence the development of animism as a religion. As food gathering was replaced by agriculture in early man, the gods of the hunter were replaced by the gods of the farmer. In every community, there were "medicine men, or witch doctors"[6] who performed magic spells and acts. The object of these practices was to influence nature and thereby increase the likelihood of a bountiful harvest.

As religious practices developed, the spiritual side of man became more personalized and the concept of a soul developed. Every person has a soul, which is the unique and individualized aspect of their spirit. The soul is the nonphysical part of personhood- the emotions, intellect and will.[7] In the Hebrew Bible, the term indicated "not only the entire inner nature of man, but also his entire personality."[8] In the Christian Bible, the Greek word for soul "has the simple meaning of life" and "an essence which differs from the body, and is not dissolved by death."[9] The Greek word for soul also means "the seat of the feelings, desires, affections [and] aversions."[10]

The Christian theologian, St. Augustine, believed that the soul and spirit were synonymous, because in the Christian Bible the terms often were used interchangeably and had the same functions. But there are sometimes subtle differences. For example, a person's soul may be "lost" but the spirit is never in that condition.[11]

In a non-Christian context the soul had a different meaning. It meant the essence of a person without necessarily implying a spiritual or immortal side. This concept was found in the writings of Plato.

THE FORMULATION OF PLATO

Plato described the soul of man as having three parts- what we would call today mind, body and spirit. The first part, the mind " was the part with which a man gains knowledge and understanding."[12] If this dominates a person, they are part of a class of men Plato called "the philosophie."[13] The second part of the soul, the body, Plato called the appetite, "because of the intensity of the appetites connected with eating...drinking and sex."[14] Persons in which this trait was dominant were called "lovers of pleasure."[15] The third element in man, the spirit, is "wholly bent on winning power and victory and a good name. So we might call it honour-loving or ambitious."[16] Persons dominated by this trait were called "the ambitious."[17]

For Plato, mind, body and spirit were the essence of a person. The mind and body were described in terms similar to what we use today. But, the spirit did not have the immortal properties or the characteristics of the soul which have been described. The spiritual side of man had these properties in civilizations before and after ancient Greece, but they did not appear in Plato's spirit.

The value of Plato, for this book, lies not so much in his discussion of mind, body and spirit, as in their implications for social institutions. In *The Republic*, Plato wrote that the three parts of man were an inspiration for the three parts of government which man created. He wrote "*we must admit that the same elements and characters that appear in the state must exist in every one of us; where else could they have come from?"*[18] (italics mine). Our ideas of government come from our conceptions of self- mind, body and spirit.

Plato believed that the three chief social functions of the state were "deliberative and governing, executive, and productive."[19] In order for justice to prevail in the state, these functions had to be performed correctly and kept distinct from one another. In every state the three functions were present, but their relative strength varied from state to state, i.e. the executive function could be stronger in one state than in another. Plato found this to be an exact parallel to the individual, where one of the three aspects of the soul tended to predominate.

In our modern conception of the state, the three branches and functions of government are the executive, legislative and judicial. In many ways they are parallel to Plato's functions of the state. The executive is an exact parallel, representing the force which "executes" laws in the state. The legislative branch of government performs very much like Plato's "deliberative and governing" aspect of the state. Congress deliberates over new laws and is the ultimate governing authority in the United States. The U.S. Constitution clearly gives the most powerful role in governing to the legislative branch. The judicial branch seems to have no parallel in Plato's "productive" function of the state, since the courts resolve legal disputes and arbitrate between conflicting parties. Perhaps the judicial function is a more modern development in the state which reflects the growth of human rights and the property rights for individuals.

Plato's formulation clearly establishes the link between our perceptions of self and our conceptions of how the state should function. Plato said that the social functions of the state were created from elements in our soul, what we would called today our "self." It is the thesis of this book that many of our conceptions in the social sciences, and perhaps in all branches of knowledge, are based on this knowledge of ourselves. Therefore it is important that we begin with a clear understanding of the nature of mind, body and spirit, and our perceptions of them.

THE MIND

The mind is the human organism which directs activities. It gains knowledge, develops understanding and uses its abilities to guide the body and spirit in their activities. David Hume in *A Treatise of Human Nature* observed that the activities of the mind consist of impressions and ideas. He wrote that impressions are "all our sensations, passions and emotions, as they make their first appearance in the soul."[20] So impressions are more primal than ideas, and are imbued with emotion and passion. Ideas are "the faint images of these [impressions] in thinking and reasoning."[21] Impressions aid the thought process, but are transformed into ideas by thinking and reasoning. Hume appears to give equal importance to reason and emotion as the activities of the mind.

Plato believed the mind was the "deliberative and governing"[22] part of the soul. Similarly, Aristotle believed it "to be an independent substance implanted within the soul" which was "incapable of being destroyed."[23] The mind, unlike the brain, was immortal for Aristotle. The brain is the physical organ which makes the activities of the mind possible, but after the body dies the mind continues as part of the soul. Evidently the mind receives power to continue its activities from another source.

Religion teaches that the other source is God. If God is the creator and sustainer of all things, then he sustains the human mind after death. The human mind was a critical proof of the existence of God, for John Stuart Mill. He wrote "it is self evident that nothing can have produced mind but mind."[24] The human mind is such a remarkable instrument that nothing but a higher intelligence could have created it.

Albert Einstein believed that God's creation is the best explanation for the existence of mankind. He wrote "I believe in...God, who reveals himself in the harmony of all being," and "I defend the Good God against the idea of a continuous game of dice."[25] Einstein wrote that the harmony of natural law "reveals an intelligence of such superiority that, compared with it, all systematic thinking and acting of human beings is an utterly insignificant reflection."[26]

Since God created man with a mind, a reflection of his own intelligence, the mind may be a key to understanding God. It is certainly a key to understanding his creation. I believe that the mind acts as a template, shaping human knowledge, and the mind is an archetype for particular aspects of knowledge in the social sciences.

An archetype is an "original model or type after which other similar things are patterned; a prototype."[27] Transforming Plato's terms, the mind is an archetype for that aspect of government involved in deliberation and governing. In modern terms, we might call that aspect the legislative process. Legislators deliberate over new laws, much as the mind deliberates over courses of action. They also govern a nation by making laws which direct its course, much as the mind governs the body and directs its actions.

The word "archetype" often is associated in modern thinking with the work of C.G. Jung. In Jung's work, *Archetypes of the Collective Unconscious*, archetypes are based on myths and fairy tales found in an individual's culture. The archetype is "a symbolical formula, which...begins to function whenever there are no conscious ideas present."[28] Jung wrote that the non-psychological forms of archetypes are simple patterns used to guide different forms of human activity. They are conscious thoughts which direct human activity by providing a model.

The mind is an archetype for various concepts in the social sciences. In political science, it is an archetype for the legislative process. But, it also influences economics, psychology, sociology and anthropology. Those influences will be discussed in detail in subsequent chapters.

But, to return to the mind and its essential characteristics, understanding the human mind has always been a challenge to scholars. It is not simply the domain of psychology or biology- most social science disciplines attempt to understand the mind. One anthropologist writes, "Laying a foundation for understanding human nature and, hence, the human mind is the single most important unfinished piece of business in the social sciences today."[29] He also writes that the "future of human biology most of interest to anthropology is the human mind."[30]

What is the mind? It is "a very complex combination of specialized mechanisms."[31] As Hume mentioned, the mind has the essential functions of reason and emotion. But it also is capable of imagination, memory, speech, consciousness, and other inexplicable phenomena. It is a marvel of engineering and creation.

Speech is "one of the most essential elements "[32] of civilization, and in fact civilization would not have been possible without it. But the origin of speech and how it developed is a mystery. Even the great philologists "are forced to either avoid the subject altogether, or to turn themselves into metaphysicians in order to discuss it."[33]

The mind will always contain mysterious properties, beyond the explanation of science. But one thing is clear- the mind, while man is alive, always operates in conjunction with the body. As the mind goes, so goes the body. The literature in health indicates that the treatment of the mind often involves treatment of the body, and vice versa.[34] The mind resides in the body and cannot function without its aid.

THE BODY

John Locke wrote that a "sound mind in a sound body is a short, but full description of a happy state in this world."[35] Today our thinking about the human body has become increasingly complex, as we gain more knowledge about its operation from medical research. The body can be thought of as a group of systems which operate to sustain life and health, e.g. the circulatory system, the digestive system, and the nervous system.

The body also may be thought of in terms of its genetic structure. With the discovery of DNA and more recent studies of the human genome, research has discovered potential cures for many illnesses. DNA evidence has transformed criminal justice, and made identification of potential criminals virtually a fool-proof process. And research into human genetic structure will develop cures in the future for diseases ranging from obesity to cancer.

Our concept of the body also is an archetype in the social sciences. Human beings view their bodies as mechanisms for accomplishing tasks. Our mind conceives of a plan and our body carries it out. The body contains the power and strength to make dreams a reality, or simply to carry on day-to-day activities. The body executes the will of its director, the mind, whether it be the simple task of drinking a glass of water or the complex task of pursuing a career.

The word "execute" is useful because it shows how the body is an archetype in political science. Plato mentions the "executive" as one of the three social functions of the state. The executive represents the physical force of the state in carrying out its laws and decrees. Today we would say the executive branch of government exercises power to enforce the law, protect society and ensure the administration of justice. If the body is an archetype for the executive branch of government, then a further understanding of the body may help in directing the activities of government wisely.

The body is best understood in its totality when viewed from the perspective of health. Health is a concept that illustrates the body in operation, performing it functions well. The concept of health is relatively new in recorded history. References to health in the English language began appearing about 1000 A.D. and referred to wholeness or soundness.[36] Initially health was conceptualized as body, mind and spirit, and only later in the 18th century did the definition become more limited to physical health and the absence of disease or illness.

But health has been a concern of man since his self-awareness, and it can be inferred that health always has been perceived as mind, body and spirit. In tribal cultures, most healers were priests who healed both the body and spirit.[37] Mind and spirit also were linked, as priests often were teachers who approached health in a holistic way.

Today health is viewed in at least four different ways. The medical model views health as the absence of disease or disability.[38] One is healthy if the negative influences can be avoided- chronic and acute illness and disability. The model is well-suited to medicine because medicine focuses on attacking and eliminating disease and its consequences. Partly because the medical sector is the most influential group in society addressing health issues, the medical model is the most popular definition of health today.

Another popular model of health is that of the World Health Organization (WHO). The WHO defines health as "a state of complete physical, mental and social well-being, and not merely the absence of disease or infirmity."[39] This model specifically rejects the medical model which stresses an absence of disease or infirmity, and it defines health in three dimensions- physical, mental and social well-being. There is no mention of the spiritual, which is replaced by "social" well-being. The WHO model is more complete than the medical model, but it rejects the traditional way of viewing health as mind, body and spirit.

Why does it reject spiritual health in favor of social health? I think there are at least two reasons. First, when the WHO model was formulated in 1947 the world was recovering from World War II, which caused many to question why such a war could occur. The lack of health in societies and social health in individuals was postulated as a possible cause, and hence its importance to the WHO.[40] Specifically, the social health of Germany, Italy and Japan were called into question.

Another reason for abandoning the idea of spiritual health was simply the difficulty of measuring it. The "validity of the spiritual dimension of health is dependent not only upon one's belief in the existence of spiritual forces, but one's beliefs concerning the particular nature and manner of functioning of these forces."[41] So partly for this reason, and despite the popularity of a spiritual dimension in human thinking, "the framers of the WHO definition chose to ignore the issue completely."[42]

The third model of health is the wellness model. The term wellness may have come from the WHO idea of well-being, but its origin is unclear. The wellness model focuses on "excellence in health and progress toward a future state of health."[43] In terms of bodily health it implies "comfort, energy, and ability to perform."[44] Wellness is a state of higher functioning where the body, mind and spirit are completely integrated and complementary to each other's functioning.

The fourth model is the environmental model. It defines heath as "the perfect continuing adjustment of an organism to its environment."[45] This definition implies a harmony with one's environment, which leads to freedom from physical pain and discomfort. It also implies positive benefits such as personal growth, happiness and rewarding social interaction. So it applies to mind and spirit as well as body.

The Spirit

The spirit is the element in man which is eternal. Aristotle calls the spirit the "soul," believing that the "soul holds the body together" and " when the soul departs the body disintegrates and decays."[46] For Aristotle, the mind is "incapable of being destroyed,"[47] so it joins the immortal soul when the body dies.

In the writings of Plato, the spirit is part of the soul but it is not eternal. The spirited element in man is "bent upon winning power and victory and a good name. So we might call it honour-loving or ambitious."[48] For Plato the spirit is a secular entity which enables man to be successful on earth, in fact, men in which the spirited element predominates are called ambitious.

But traditionally the spirit has been endowed with eternal properties. As mentioned earlier, the idea of the spirit existed in tribal societies where priests were healers, and in the Middle Ages where health as mind, body and spirit was first written about in the English language.

Our conception of spirit is an important archetype in the social sciences. In political science, it is an archetype for judicial functioning. The spirit, like the judiciary, is able to make moral judgments and find just solutions to problems. The mind responds to the promptings of the spirit, but it is the spirit itself which makes these judgments.

St. Thomas Acquinas believed that justice and morality were intimately related, and were *not* a product of human reason. He wrote that "justice is not an intellectual virtue," but rather " it is a moral virtue."[49] To be just means "rectifying a man's operations in relation to another man." Or to quote Isidore "a man is said to be just because he respects the rights"[50] of others.

Hume also recognized that moral judgments did not come from reason. He wrote that moral distinctions are "not derived from reason," but morality "is more properly felt than judged of."[51] Hume believed that the emotions made moral distinctions and contributed to our sense of justice. He wrote that the sense of justice in man came from "the selfishness and confin'd generosity of men, along with the scanty provision nature has made for his wants."[52] In other words, justice is necessary because of man's natural selfishness and the shortage of economic goods.

Hume believed that the emotions, rather than the spirit, provided moral judgments. The seat of the emotions, in Western cultures, is the heart. In the Christian faith, the heart is considered the source of moral judgments as well. Jesus said " the mouth speaks out of that which fills the heart".[53] So where does the spirit come in?

Jesus tells his disciples at one point "the spirit is willing, but the flesh is weak."[54] The spirit is a strong directing force in one's life, encouraging the body when it is weak. The book of Luke says that Jesus as a "child continued to grow, and to become strong in the spirit."[55] The spirit can grow and be stronger in some persons than in others. And the Apostle Paul writes that Christians should be "of the same mind, maintaining the same love, united in spirit, intent on one purpose."[56] The spirit can be united with purpose in life, indicating a moral force or direction.

It appears that the heart can do good or evil, but the spirit directs toward good behavior, at least from the Christian perspective. The spirit directs the heart to make correct judgments and pursue the right course of action. So the spirit is the originating force for morality and justice, while it often uses the heart as a vehicle for expressing those sentiments.

The linkage between the spirit and the heart, or the emotions, is further demonstrated by its role in the conversion to religious faith. Conversion in the Christian faith is more an experience of the heart than of the reasoning faculty of the mind. The Christian Bible says that spiritual truths are spiritually discerned, so the avenue toward understanding spiritual matters is primarily through the heart. Blaise Pascal, the French philosopher and scientist, expresses this truth eloquently when he writes that the heart has reasons that reason knows nothing of.

The heart and spirit also are connected in the teachings of Judaism. The Shema, or the greatest commandment of the Hebrew Bible, says in part "you shall love the Lord your God with all your heart and with all your soul and with all your might."[57] The heart is listed first as an essential element of faith and a means by which we reach and worship the Spirit of God.

So the spirit speaks to the heart and is the source of justice and moral judgments. It judges between right and wrong, good and evil, fair and unfair. Often its judgments are quick, even as the emotions are quick. But sometimes the judgments are slow, as complex facts must be sorted through before moral judgments can be made.

The spirit is an archetype for the judicial branch in our political system. The linkage between the spirit and judicial functioning is clear when the spirit is linked with morality and justice. The essence of judicial functioning is fairness and impartiality in judging disputes between parties. That fairness is ensured, in the U.S. system, by a judiciary that is independent of outside forces which may cause bias. Our legal system also is governed by rules and precedents which ensure that all parties are treated fairly. These rules and precedents are a form of codified morality that guarantees consistent and just treatment of parties coming before the judiciary.

In the next chapter, judicial and other aspects of government will be discussed more fully. Mind, body and spirit are the source of these ideas and influence the continuing evolution of political science and the social sciences. They are the archetypes for knowledge in the social sciences. Table 1 summarizes the basic elements in the theory of archetypes.

Table 1. Elements of the Theory of Archetypes

Mind The directive force, guiding the body and making decisions for the benefit of the body and spirit. The mind contains rational thought, logic, emotions, memory, imagination, and numerous other qualities. In the theory of archetypes, it should be subservient to the spirit. *Body* The physical force, exerting power over its environment, and carrying out the directions of the mind. The body often is guided by habits, which originate with decisions by the mind, but often have an influence all their own. While the body is subservient to the mind, it provides vital input that affects the mind's decisions. *Spirit* The corrective force, which provides moral and ethical guidance to the mind and body. The spirit should be the most powerful force in human activities, but it also must restrain itself from interfering too frequently with the activities of the mind and body. Such interference can cause dysfunction.

CONCLUSIONS

The purpose of this book is to develop a new theory for the social sciences. Large-scale theories in the social sciences are not common. Behaviorism is an example of one, as it has influenced psychology, political science and other social sciences. Mid-level theories are much more common, but their shortcoming is that they generally apply only within one discipline. In this book, five social science disciplines are examined- politics, economics, psychology, sociology and anthropology. My apologies to those disciplines which have been ignored, but these seem to be the major disciplines in the social sciences.

I have alluded already to the application of the theory of archetypes to politics. (I will use the abbreviated term politics instead of political science). The theory of archetypes applied to politics says that the mind is an archetype for legislative functioning, the body for executive functioning, and the spirit for judicial functioning. Now the theory will be fleshed out, so that eventually hypotheses can be developed. The testing of these hypotheses over time will help to determine the validity of the theory.

The theory of archetypes says that man's social institutions and behavior are derived from the perceptions of his own mind, body and spirit. As those perceptions change over time, so do the institutions inspired by them. It is a dynamic process, even though the foundations are based on the simple triad.

The theory also says that the archetypes of mind, body and spirit form an ideal, which is a pattern for social institutions to follow. Ideally, mind, body and spirit are in balance and each performs specific functions. When those functions are not in balance and do not properly complement each other, human health suffers. Similarly when the three elements in various social institutions are not in balance, then society suffers.

This leads to another use of the theory of archetypes. It can be used to diagnose and treat social ills, drawing from our knowledge of the proper relationships between mind, body and spirit. In politics, for instance, when the executive branch is too powerful it is like the body overwhelming the mind and spirit. If the executive branch dominates to the point of dictatorship, the state becomes brutal, unjust and lacking in proper enforcement of laws and policies. Eventually the state suffers and dies for lack of proper direction and the right moral compass.

As hypotheses are tested, another aspect of the theory will become more clear. It will shed light on two questions concerning the theory. Are the social institutions which come from the three archetypes a product of man's conscious (or unconscious) thinking alone? Or is there a pattern in nature which guides the whole process, which contains these three elements in balance? Some evidence from science and the natural world indicates that the latter question may be answered affirmatively. As mentioned earlier, certain groups of phenomena in nature come in "threes." All matter is either solid, liquid or gas; the primary colors in the spectrum of light are red, blue and yellow; and atoms consist of protons, neutrons and electrons. A triad seems to exist in nature among certain phenomena.

Finally, the theory of archetypes may be useful in diagnosing subtle dysfunctions in society. This chapter has spent some time discussing essential elements in the mind, body and spirit. Their functioning and interaction may give interesting insights into the operation of major social institutions. For example, in the executive branch of government administrators perform routine tasks of government. Similarly, the body performs many of its routine tasks from habit, which makes performance of those tasks easier. Studying the body and the nature of habits, may shed light on the role of administration in the executive branch. New insight into problems in administration may come from a more complete understanding of the role of habits in helping the body to perform its functions.

NOTES

[1] www.threes.com
[2] Alan Dundes. "The Number Three in American Culture." In Alan Dundes (Ed.) *Every Man His Way: Readings in Cultural Anthropology*. (Englewood Cliffs, NJ: Prentice Hall, 1966), 419.
[3] Ibid, 402.
[4] Tom B. Jones. *Ancient Civilzation*. (Chicago: Rand McNally & Co., 1960), 14.
[5] Ibid., 14.
[6] Ibid., 21.
[7] Dallas Willard. "Gray matter and the soul, *Christianity Today*, 46:12, 74.
[8] Merrill F. Unger. *Unger's Bible Dictionary*. (Chicago: Moody Press, 1966), 1040.
[9] Ibid., 1040.
[10] Ibid., 1040.
[11] Ibid., 1040.
[12] Francis M. Cornford. *The Republic of Plato*. (London: Oxford University Press, 1970), 306.
[13] Ibid., 307.
[14] Ibid., 306.
[15] ibid., 307.
[16] Ibid., 306.
[17] Ibid., 307.
[18] Ibid., 132.
[19] Ibid., 129.
[20] David Hume. *A Treatise of Human Nature*. (Baltimore: Penguin, 1969), 49.
[21] Ibid., 49.
[22] Cornford, op. cit., 129.
[23] Richard McKeon (Ed.). *Introduction to Aristotle*. (New York: The Modern Library, 1947), 163.
[24] Michael Caputo. *God Seen Through the Eyes of the Greatest Minds*. (West Monroe, LA: Howard Publishing, 2000), 58.
[25] Ibid., 80-81.
[26] Ibid., 81.
[27] *The American Heritage Dictionary, Second College Edition*. (Boston: Houghton Mifflin, 1985), 125.
[28] Violet DeLaszlo (Ed.). *The Basic Writings of C.G. Jung*. (New York: The Modern Library, 1959), 220.
[29] Donald Brown. *Human Universals*. (Philadelphia: Temple University Press, 1991),
[30] Ibid., 6.
[31] Ibid., 144.
[32] Sir Edward Burnett Tylor. *Researches into the Early History of Mankind and the Development of Civilization*. (Chicago: University of Chicago Press, 1964), 9.
[33] Ibid., 10.
[34] Martha O. Loustaunau. *The Cultural Concept of Health, Illness, and Medicine*. (Westport, CT: Bergin & Garvey, 1997), 86.
[35] Maurice Cranston (Ed.) *Locke on Politics, Religion, and Education*. (New York: Collier Books, 1965), 149.
[36] Bruce Simons-Morton et al. *Introduction to Health Education and Promotion, 2nd Edition*. (Prospect Heights, IL: Waveland Press, 1995), 6.
[37] Paul Solomon. "The Triune Concept." In Peter Albright and Bets Albright (Eds.) *Body, Mind & Spirit: The Journey Toward Health and Wholeness*. (Brattleboro, VT: Greene Press, 1980), 82.
[38] James S. Larson. *The Measurement of Health: Concepts and Indicators*. (New York: Greenwood Press, 1991), 3.
[39] Ian McDowell and Claire Newell. *Measuring Health: A Guide to Rating Scales and Questionnaires*. (New York: Oxford University Press, 1987), 14.

[40] James S. Larson. "The world health organization's definition of health: Social versus spiritual health," *Social Indicators Research*, 38:2 (June 1996), 181-192.
[41] Simon-Morton et al., op. cit., 8.
[42] Ibid., 8.
[43] Larson, *The Measurement of Health*, op. cit., 3.
[44] Ann Greer. "The measurement of health in urban communities," *Journal of Urban Affairs*, 8 (Spring 1986), 11.
[45] Seth Goldsmith. "The status of health indicators," *Health Services Reports*, 87:3 (March 1972), 213.
[46] McKeon, op.cit., 163.
[47] Ibid., 163.
[48] Cornford, op.cit., 307.
[49] Dino Bigongiari. *The Political Ideas of St. Thomas Aquinas*. (New York: Hafner, 1969), 111.
[50] Ibid., 106.
[51] Hume, op. cit., 522.
[52] Ibid., 54.
[53] *New American Standard Bible*. (Nashville: Holman Bible Publishers, 1977), Matthew 12:34, 10.
[54] Ibid., Matthew 26:41, 24.
[55] Ibid., Luke 1:80, 46.
[56] Ibid., Philippians 2:2, 157.
[57] *Tanakh: A New Translation of the Holy Scriptures According to the Original Hebrew Text.* (Philadelphia: The Jewish Publication Society, 1985), Deuteronomy 5:6, 284.

Chapter 2

POLITICS

The philosophers of the Enlightenment believed that before society existed man lived in a state of nature. Conservative writers like Thomas Hobbes believed that the "state of nature was a state of war,"[1] and therefore governments should be strong. Liberal and radical writers like Jean Jacques Rousseau pictured a peaceful state of nature with a "pastoral glow"[2] about it, and therefore the principal role of governments was to maximize individual liberty.

Since that time anthropologists and historians have discovered much about the condition of early man. Elman Service's model of sociopolitical evolution is particularly influential in the field of anthropology. He argues that sociopolitical evolution began with *bands of people* whose members exploited natural resources.[3] These hunters and gatherers lived off the land, hunting game and gathering berries, roots and other edibles. Food gathering was replaced by food production in the Near East around 6000 B.C.[4] Bands of people were replaced by *tribes* who were mainly cultivators of the land,[5] and agriculture brought population growth and private property.

Tribes were characterized by personal leadership and the lack of a political hierarchy. In time, this form of organization was replaced by *chiefdoms*, which developed centers to "coordinate economic, social and religious activities."[6] The village chief became a high priest who presided over religious ceremonies connected with planting, cultivation and harvesting. Church and state became unified. As villages grew, city life "made governmental organization more complex" and "made necessary the growth of bureaucracy."[7] The head of government became more remote from the common man and took on kingly characteristics. Near East Civilizations came to be ruled by a "priest-king"[8], and a priestly class developed along with social stratification.

Civilization first arose in the lower Tigris-Euphrates Valley[9] about 4000 B.C. The Sumerian civilization included a system of writing (cuneiform), a legal code, science, math, theology and other developments. There is some evidence that before their recorded history, a kind of primitive democracy existed "in which decisions were made by a council of elders or by an assembly of people."[10] But recorded history shows that the different Sumerian city states "were ruled by kings who functioned as war leaders, administrators, and intermediaries between the people and the gods."[11]

Plato, Aristotle and Hobbes equated government with civilization and assumed that precivilization was anarchic. But anthropological evidence indicates that it was not so, as "social behavior was strikingly constrained."[12] Constraints were placed on the individual by the family, by the immediate social group or tribe, and by the leadership of the decentralized group. The origins of government were "in the institutionalization of centralized leadership."[13] Over time, this leadership and its administrative functions grew into a hereditary aristocracy.

The executive function of government developed first, in the form of this leadership, but the judicial function was not far behind. With private property came methods for settling disputes and these methods ultimately became laws. Criminal acts also required a judicial function in the community, usually performed by the leader or chief. Judicial and legislative functions were subordinate to the executive, but nevertheless vital to the existence of government and society. Wittfogel argues that social systems developed from the problem of creating water control systems for cities. He writes that social systems "could only have come about through the development of bureaucratic power over the hydraulic (water-control) system."[14] Thus political power "organized the economy, and not vice versa."[15]

Executive, legislative and judicial functions were created from necessity, but their design and function were not accidental. As Plato suggested, their design and function were an imitation of man himself, of mind, body and spirit. The executive function was important first, because government needed physical force to assert itself and organize society. The judicial and legislative functions developed later, but were increasing important as society became more complex.

In this chapter the role of mind, body and spirit as archetypes for legislative, executive and judicial functioning will be explored. Since the executive function in government developed first, it is the first subject of discussion.

Body as Executive Functioning

The body consists of appetites, desires and physical force- the energy to carry out the desires of the mind and spirit. The body also can dominate the mind and spirit, as Plato believed, and the result would be persons who are lovers of pleasure.[16] Obviously harmony between mind, body and spirit is desirable. As mentioned earlier, Locke wrote that a "sound mind in a sound body is a short, but full description of a happy state in this world."[17] He did not ignore the spirit, as he believed that virtue was learned by teaching young men about a loving God who "gives us all good things"[18] and that we should emulate that goodness.

While Locke did not observe the connection between the body and executive functioning in government, he did note the need to separate executive and legislative functions. He found it necessary to have a power "always in being" that is responsible for "execution of the laws," and that such power should be "separated" from the legislative power. He noted that "several things should be left to the discretion of him that has executive power."[19] As the body executes the desires of the mind so the executive power has the physical force to require that laws be obeyed.

Alexander Hamilton, coauthor of the *Federalist Papers*, wrote of the executive as needing an "energy" necessary to the successful operation of government. Energy in executive functioning is "a leading character in the definition of good government" and it is "essential to the protection of the community against foreign attacks"[20] in particular. The executive works as a body does, following directions, executing actions, protecting mind and spirit, and at times acting independently for its own self-preservation and pleasure. The Founding Fathers protected against abuse of power by the executive through the balance and separation of powers.

Hamilton and the other Founding Fathers believed that the executive, legislative and judicial branches of government should be in proper balance to create the best government. A proper "balance of powers" was necessary for good functioning since a dominance by one branch would lead to tyranny or ineffectiveness in government. When the executive branch is too strong, tyranny is the natural outcome. When the legislative branch is too powerful, government may be too weak to protect itself and lack a sustained direction and purpose. If the judicial branch becomes overly dominant, government may suffer from a form of paralysis, being unable to act or make decisions, and lacking in innovation and new ideas.

This is just like the body and its potential dysfunctions. When the physical body (like the executive) dominates over mind and spirit, bodily comfort, pleasure and other self-seeking behaviors tend to dominate. A person who lives such a life is self-centered and lacks meaning and purpose. When the mind (like the legislature) is too dominant over body and spirit, ideas become more important than justice or compassion. Abstraction becomes more significant than reality. If the spirit (like the judiciary) is too dominant, ethics and morality are more important than enjoyment of life or the flexibility to evolve as conditions of life change. Some of the higher values of the spirit are found in the Christian ideal of the "fruits of the spirit." The Apostle Paul writes that the fruits of the spirit are: "love, joy peace, patience, kindness, goodness, faithfulness, gentleness, self-control."[21] When these values are found in a judicial system, it is optimal and the best society is formed.

Yet the mind, body and spirit should not always be in perfect balance. Ideally spirit should control mind, and the mind should dominate the body. In the political realm, the judicial functions of justice, ethics and rule of law should dominate legislative activities, guiding their function in producing laws. Legislative direction should dominate and direct the executive activities of national defense, implementation of policy, and other functions. But in emergencies the body must act independently of the mind and spirit to preserve itself. Similarly the executive must act quickly at times to preserve the nation.

Aside from the issues of balance, an important aspect of the executive branch is administration. As mentioned earlier, administration is to the executive branch what habits are to the human body. Standard operating procedures ordinarily are used to perform the duties of the executive branch. Some significant issues in the area of administration are the relationships between administrators and the political appointees in the executive branch, relationships with the other branches of government, and the desirability of a separation between politics and administration. In our political system, politics and administration are difficult to separate, although administrators are expected to carry out programs without personal political bias. The body as an archetype supplies guidelines for how administration should act within a political system.

The habitual actions of the body derive from decisions of the mind to act in certain ways. We learn how to brush our teeth through conscious effort, but the daily practice scarcely requires any conscious thought. We can be thinking about the events of the day, and be totally unaware of the act of tooth-brushing. Periodically the mind may oversee the process to be sure that things are going well, or if they are not, to interrupt the process. Similarly, the legislature may allow administrators to implement programs, but periodically hold oversight hearings to correct problems or make sure things are going well.

Administrators rarely are interrupted in their work by the judicial branch of government, but when they are it usually is to correct major problems associated with justice or equity. Similarly the spirit rarely interrupts the body in its habitual activity unless those habits become offensive to the values of the spirit. Administrators are forced by law (the mind) to obey the dictates of the judiciary.

The relationship of administrators to political appointees in the executive branch is guided by obedience to political authority. Habits cannot be performed outside of the actions of the body, and administrators cannot act for very long without the consent of political appointees. When they do, major dysfunctions occur in the body politic. The body quickly corrects habitual action which brings harm to itself, as long as it is conscious of that harm. Sometimes the mind (legislature) must instruct it.

Administrators are never totally free from the influence of politics, because politics legitimates and guides their activities. But the routine activities of administrators must be free, without constant interference from the various branches of government. Habits must be allowed to be carried out habitually, or they lose their utility to the body. They constitute the major activity of the body on a daily basis and are vital to its healthy operation.

Mind as Legislative Functioning

The mind is an archetype for legislative functioning in the modern state. St. Thomas Aquinas in *Summa Theologica* linked the reasoning aspect of the mind to laws when he wrote that "the reason of any man is competent to make laws."[22] The quality of laws may differ with the quality of reason, but every man is capable of making laws. For Aquinas both laws and reason restrained man from acting in inappropriate ways, violating the rights of others. In fact, government existed to allow the rule of law, which is a reflection of God's eternal law.

The directing and emotive power of the mind and its relationship to making laws also is emphasized in the political philosophy of Locke. Locke wrote that the "legislative power is that which has a right to direct how the force of the commonwealth shall be employed for preserving the community and the members of it".[23] He believed that the legislative power should be supreme in the state, as the mind directs and motivates the actions of the body. The best way to ensure that members of the community can live in peace together is through the rule of law, which is ensured by the supremacy of legislative power.[24]

In the *Federalist Papers*, Alexander Hamilton and James Madison concurred with Locke in noting the necessary supremacy of legislative authority in a republican form of government. But the individual legislator also must exercise reason in making laws. In their words, the "competent legislator" must exercise "upright intention" with "sound judgment" and "a certain degree of knowledge of the subjects on which he is to legislate".[25] The essence of the legislative function is good reasoning, and as the mind should control the body so the legislative authority should be dominant over the executive authorities.

The legislature ordinarily directs activities, but when the legislative branch is not governed by justice, ethics and the rule of law, the result is corruption in society. When mind (legislature) controls spirit (judiciary) important values are lost. Corrupt societies often resort to executive control to eliminate corruption, in the form of military dictatorships. Whenever proper values do not come from a strong judicial branch, the executive branch takes over.

The legislative branch makes laws through a process called policy formulation. The formulation of policy is a complex period of bargaining in which legislative committees consider the bills placed on their agendas. Just as the mind considers new items of information and new experiences in formulating its plans of action, so the legislature becomes aware of problems in society or crises that demand immediate attention. Just as the emotions influence the process of thinking and action by the mind, so emotional and volatile events create prompt action by the legislative branch of government.

The legislature also legitimizes policies which are formulated. The process of legitimization gives policies and laws the power and respect which they deserve in society. The legislature is the legitimate voice of the people, being democratically elected and serving at the pleasure of the electorate. Similarly the mind, by virtue of its authority over the body, is the legitimate director of the body's actions. To do something "without thinking" is often synonymous with a foolish action. So the legitimate course of the body's actions are directed, at least in the long-term, by policies established by the mind.

Any legislative body also must have the power to appropriate money to fund its policies. The appropriations process requires taxes and methods for collecting money, using the executive branch. The mind also has an appropriations process which is heavily dependent on the body. The mind makes decisions and plans concerning the welfare of the body and spirit, then directs the body to gather resources to fulfill that plan. As an illustration, the mind may decide that the body needs new shoes to protect its feet. It directs the body to work, save money and purchase the new shoes. The spirit may require a time of reflection to process events in life, so the mind plans for such a time and tells the body when to rest and allow reflection. Mind and spirit are especially close in their operations together.

In this analysis, knowledge of the legislative process has been used to draw parallels with similar processes in the mind. But since the mind is the archetype for legislative functions, the process certainly can be reversed. Detailed knowledge of the mind and its activities can be used to explain legislative functions with greater clarity. For instance, the interaction of memory and reasoning in the mind may aid in improving how the legislative process uses past policies to inform future action. If the best decisions of the mind are based on the analysis of memories in a certain way or a given number of memories, the best legislative policies might emulate that process.

The mind's functioning is associated with the physiology of the brain, so more detailed knowledge of the components of the brain, their functioning and interaction, might aid in improving the legislative process. Memory in the human brain is based on engrams which store information which is accessed in the future. The strength of memory is based on how frequently the engram is used. Similarly the legislative process is based on specialized committees which are knowledgeable in particular policy areas. They serve as legislative memory of certain issues and provide knowledge for intelligent judgment by the legislature as a whole. The legislature implicitly trusts the judgment of the experts in these committees in making policy decisions.

So the mind is the directing force in our lives just as the legislature is the directing force in our political system. Sometimes it is a slow, deliberative force which lags behind physical actions of the body or body politic, but it determines the overall direction and movement of the body. Yet the mind is not alone in this process. The spirit is an element which influences the mind and forces it to dwell on issues of moral and ethical import.

Spirit as Judicial Functioning

In the writings of Plato the spirit is a part of the soul, yet it is not eternal. But traditionally the spirit has been endowed with eternal properties, as the idea of the spirit in man existed in primitive societies. People in hunting societies believed that their health was "partly dependent on respect for animal spirits that govern their lives."[26] The animal spirits released more game which allowed them to continue to eat. Primitive societies also believed almost universally that illness was the result of hostile action by a supernatural being.[27] The development of primitive art found in caves was "closely associated with a belief in magic."[28] Primitive man believed that other creatures and objects "were endowed with spirits like themselves."[29]

In traditional societies today the medical systems also are related to religious concepts. Disease often is seen as punishment for violating taboos or social rules, and the proscribed therapy is confession of one's sins. Anthropologists have discovered in American Indian tribes that "confession works as cathartic therapy"[30] for the wrongdoer. Confession is used today in the Catholic Church for that and other religious purposes.

In ancient civilizations, beliefs in spirits and the afterlife differed substantially. The early Sumerian civilization recorded no belief in life after death while the ancient Egyptians recorded such beliefs in great detail. The Egyptians believed that the afterlife was dependent on a good life on earth and was associated with moral behavior.[31]

The spirit, as it is understood today, has eternal properties as well as other aspects. In the Judeo-Christian tradition a spiritual life is a moral one and a life characterized by the just treatment of others. In fact, spirit is associated with moral judgments in most religious faiths.

If the spirit is associated with morality and justice, it is a clear archetype for judicial functioning in the state. Quarrels and disputes are "as old as mankind, or older."[32] The traditional view of the administration of justice is that individuals waived methods of self-help and resorted to arbitration. But evidence from ancient Greece indicates that the state struggled to get individuals from using revenge and other self-help methods. The state had to "hold back the fight until the conflict could be solved by judicial decision."[33]

Judicial functioning is based on the fair and impartial judging of disputes between parties. In the U.S. system, it is based on an independent judiciary which is insulated from political pressure and personal influence. The Founding Fathers sought to ensure an independent judicial system which made decisions based on objective standards. Hamilton wrote in the *Federalist Papers* that the "independence of judges is...requisite to guard the Constitution and the rights of individuals."[34] And to further prevent bias and arbitrary discretion in the courts "it is indispensable that they should be bound by strict rules and precedents."[35]

In the U.S. legal system common law is practiced, which is based on precedent. The courts are guided by previous decisions in other cases in making their own decisions to ensure fairness to all parties. Only in rare cases do judges overturn precedent and establish new precedent. Other legal systems practice code law as opposed to common law. Code law is based on written codes of law established by the legislature and followed by the courts. The most famous example of code law is the Napoleonic Code in France, which has been in force for over 200 years. In a sense the U.S. system combines common law and code law in that common law prevails in judicial decisions, but there are codes of law which are written by the legislatures. Both federal and state legislatures produce codes of laws or statutes which pertain to both civil and criminal law.

Both common law and code law are derived from the spirit of man. In the Judeo-Christian tradition, the law of Moses came from God and established a code of law by which man was to live. The Jewish law, the *Torah*, is the first five books of the Christian Bible. Since Jews and Christians believe that this law came from God, and was transmitted to man through spiritual communion with God, obviously it has spiritual origins.

Common law also has spiritual origins, in that both the Hebrew and Christian Bibles mention the judgment of cases based on God's law and man's application of it. In the Jewish tradition, extensive commentaries on the *Torah* were developed for such purpose. From the Christian perspective these commentaries were not always reflective of the original meaning of God's laws, and this became a major point of dispute between Jesus and the Pharisees in the New Testament. But the point is that precedent was used to judge disputes between parties, and this precedent has its origins in man's spirit striving to interpret God's laws.

The substance of the law also has spiritual origins. As mentioned previously, in the Christian tradition the Apostle Paul writes that the fruits of the spirit are love, joy, peace, etc. But the opposite of that is the "deeds of the flesh" which are "immorality, impurity, sensuality, idolatry, sorcery, enmities, strife, jealousy, outbursts of anger, disputes, dissensions, factions, envying, drunkenness, carousing, and things like these."[36]

The flesh or the body when ungoverned by the spirit has these natural tendencies, and these are obviously a source of unlawful behavior.

In a society in which the fruits of the spirit are dominant, citizens are restrained from unlawful behavior (or even thinking about it) by the spiritual commands to show love, patience and other good qualities. In the society where the deeds of the flesh are ungoverned by the spirit, the citizens are inclined toward immorality, strife, disputes and other evil qualities. The judicial system is a pleasure to administer in the former but a hellish task in the latter. Most societies lie on a continuum between the two extremes depending upon the penetration of spirit in that society.

CONCLUSIONS

Table 2 summarizes the application of the theory of archetypes to politics.

Table 2. Politics and the Theory of Archetypes

Mind/Legislature The legislature is like the mind, because it directs the affairs of state. As the mind directs the body, the legislature makes policy that is executed by the executive branch. Legislative actions are subject to judicial oversight. *Body/Executive* The executive is like the body, because it is a powerful physical force in the state. Its actions are directed by the legislature, but it has discretionary power to act in emergencies. The executive provides input to the legislature, as the body does for the mind, and should be an energetic force. *Spirit/Judiciary* The judiciary is like the spirit, because it provides moral and ethical guidance to the state. It should be the ultimate authority and the most powerful force in the state, but it should use its power sparingly and avoid undue interference with governmental functioning.

Since the time of Plato, man has been aware that his mind, body and spirit serve as models or archetypes for the principal functions of government. From this analysis it is concluded that the best societies are those in which a strong judiciary is dominant over the legislature, and the legislature is dominant over the executive. This dominance is not a matter of volume or frequency of activity, in fact, political systems must have executive functions which are more numerous that legislative actions, with judicial actions being the least frequent. Rather the dominance must come in deferring to the wishes of the judiciary when they are in conflict with the desires of the legislative or executive branches. In the best political systems, judicial values reflecting justice, morality and freedom must prevail.

The best forms of judicial systems are ones which best reflect the values which God has imparted to man. When societies lose their spiritual moorings, their justice systems decline and the societies decline. The success of a political system and of a society are directly linked to the spiritual values which are legally enforced by the judiciary. If that enforcement strays from the truth and it is not corrected, that society is in serious trouble. If citizens insist that proper spiritual values are enforced by government, and especially the judiciary, society will greatly benefit.

Legislative functions must be subject to judicial control and direction, but the daily business of legislatures should be governed by clear thinking and intelligent deliberation. The best legislatures combine knowledgeable members with a will to represent the wishes of the people. In the previous chapter, the health of the body was analyzed with the environmental model of health. Just as the body adapts to its changing environment, so the legislature must adapt to changing social, political and economic environments to be healthy.

Legislatures operate best when they accurately perceive the environment and respond accordingly. This requires not only the best information available but also the most intelligent analysis. Good information comes from good relations with the executive branch, which collects information as a regular part of its functioning. Just as a healthy body collects good information for the mind to use in regulating the activities of the body, so the properly functioning executive cooperates with the legislature to provide the best information to make policies.

When the executive branch is operating at its best, it is cooperating with the legislature and also playing a subordinate role. It recognizes that the best policy comes from the deliberations of a democratically elected body and so it yields to the wisdom of that body. The executive branch should view itself with humility, even though it has great powers and can force its will on the legislature. The chief executive is largely responsible for the tone of the executive branch, whether it has an attitude of arrogance or humility.

In the wellness model of health, the body is described as progressing toward higher states of health. It increases its level of energy, comfort and well-being as it cooperates more with the mind and spirit. The executive branch functions best when it develops a symbiotic relationship with the rest of government; seeking to advance the goals of the legislative and judicial branches, it raises the level of its own performance. The health of the body politic is directly related to how well the executive branch cooperates with its partners in government.

NOTES

1 Adam Kuper. *The Chosen Primate: Human Nature and Cultural Diversity*. (Cambridge: Harvard University Press, 1994), 208.

2 Ibid., 208.

3 Henri J.M. Claessen and Pieter van de Velde. "The Evolution of Sociopolitical Organizations," in *Development and Decline: The Evolution of Sociopolitical Organization*. Henri J.M. Claessen, Pieter van de Velde and M Estellie Smith (Eds.). (South Hadley, MA: Bergin & Garvey Publishers, 1985), 133.

[4] Tom B. Jones. *Ancient Civilization.* (Chicago: Rand McNally & Co., 1960), 18.
[5] Claessen and van de Velde, op. cit., 133.
[6] Ibid., 133.
[7] Jones, op. cit., 31.
[8] Ibid., 31.
[9] Ibid., 40.
[10] Ibid., 45.
[11] Ibid., 45.
[12] Elman R. Service. *Origins of the State and Civilization: The Process of Cultural Evolution.* (New York: Norton, 1975), 5.
[13] Ibid., 8.
[14] Ibid., 273.
[15] Ibid.
[16] Francis M. Cornford (Ed.). *The Republic of Plato.* (London: Oxford University Press, 1970), 307.
[17] Maurice Cranston (Ed.). *Locke on Politics, Religion, and Education.* (New York: Collier Books, 1965), 149.
[18] Ibid., 205
[19] John Locke. *Second Treatise of Civil Government.* (Chicago: Gateway, 1955), 135.
[20] Alexander Hamilton, John Jay and James Madison. *The Federalist.* (New York: Modern Library, 1787), 454.
[21] *New American Standard Bible.* (Nashville: Holman Bible Publishers, 1977), 152 (Galatians 5:22-23).
[22] Dino Bigongiari. *The Political Ideas of St.Thomas Aquinas.* (New York: Hafner, 1969), 4.
[23] Locke, op. cit., 120.
[24] Cranston, op. cit., 64.
[25] Hamilton et al., op. cit., 349.
[26] Colin Samson (Ed.). *Health Studies: A Critical and Cross-Cultural Reader.* (Oxford: Blackwell Publishers, 1999), 77.
[27] George Murdock. *Theories of Illness: A World Survey.* (Pittsburgh: University of Pittsburgh Press, 1980), 72.
[28] Jones, op. cit., 14.
[29] Ibid., 14.
[30] Erika Bourguignon. *Psychological Anthropology: An Introduction to Human Nature and Cultural Differences.* (New York: Holt, Rinehart and Winston, 1971), 288.
[31] Henry O. Taylor. *Ancient Ideals, Volume II, 2nd Ed.* (New York: MacMillan Co., 1930), 17.
[32] Rolando Tamyo y Salmoran. "The Judicial Litigation in Early Stages and the Evolution of the Legal Process," in Claessen et al., op. cit., 313.
[33] Ibid., 320.
[34] Hamilton et al, op. cit., 508.
[35] Ibid., 510.
[36] *New American Standard Bible*, op. cit., 152 (Galatians 5: 19-21).

Chapter 3

ECONOMICS

It is relatively simple to imagine the economic exchanges that took place in the time of pre-civilization. Early man probably traded everything from food and clothing to tools and primitive handicrafts. Today, studies of aboriginal societies without governments find that "ceremonial exchanges"[1] take place using things like shell bracelets and other valuables. The purpose of such exchanges is to form alliances in warfare, peacemaking, marriage and other ceremonies. Sometimes human beings also are traded in marriage for these purposes.[2]

Although no one is certain, the use of money, rather than barter, probably began with early civilizations. Civilization also signaled the beginning of governmental regulation of economic activity to ensure fairness, efficiency, legality and other desirable outcomes. In the Babylonian Code of Hammurabi, archeologists found "detailed regulations for economic activity"[3] in the Sumerian civilization. As civilization developed, states became more involved in the details of economic life. In ancient Greece, Plato notes that economic production "is the basis of the state,"[4] implying that the state could not exist without a prior foundation in economic activity. Furthermore, the specialization of economic activities and a "diversity of occupations"[5] makes a political community necessary. The state must exist to allow the orderly exchange of goods and services.

Aristotle based his economic theories on the management of a household. Economic functions in the state should be governed by the principles of honesty, frugality and balancing expenditure with income. He heartily disapproved of the use of currency and lending money for interest, because he believed it tempted people to accumulate wealth. Aristotle believed that that was counterproductive in a just society, as it promoted "disparity in riches and financial irregularities."[6]

In the Middle Ages, economic activity became more sophisticated and more organized. Many merchants and craftsmen organized into guilds, which are somewhat like trade associations in business today. The guilds established "standards of skill, the prices of purchase and sale, and rates of wages."[7] Governmental authorities continued to regulate economic activity, but the Christian Church "vied with temporal authorities for power and strove to impose a moral order on the institutions of the time."[8] The Church supported a "just wage and fair price"[9] for laborers and merchants as a part of their economic doctrine.

In time, cities grew larger and business activity expanded, increasing trade between regional areas. The nation-state emerged as means to protect citizens and their economic interests. The state "encouraged groups of businessmen by subsidies and grants of monopoly. It protected the infant industries against foreign competition."[10] The Age of Mercantilism began. Mercantilist nations protected their merchants by imposing tariffs on the products of other nations, and engaged in other protectionist practices. Mercantilism continued as the dominant practice until Adam Smith successful refuted its wisdom in *The Wealth of Nations*. Smith's theories signaled the beginning of modern economics.

In this brief review of economic history, several points are relevant to the theory of archetypes. First, some form of government regulation is necessary for economic exchanges to occur. Regulation provides a basis for fairness in exchanges, protecting all parties involved and encouraging efficient production. Government acts as a moral agent, much as the Christian church did in the Middle Ages, to ensure correct practices and that the laws are upheld.

The theory of archetypes says that the spirit is the moral agent in man which directs human activities. Therefore, government regulation in the economic sphere is like the spirit in man. It promotes fairness, morality and the overall success of the economic system for all individuals. An important part of government regulation is taxation, so this chapter will discuss its role in ensuring fairness and efficiency in the system, as well as some of the dysfunctions of taxation.

Second, the practice of using "prices" to gauge the value of commodities has been used since the development of civilization and a monied economy. Aristotle did not like the idea of a monied economy, but he acknowledged that money was necessary to allow economic exchanges to occur. The prices of goods and services have been a driving force in the determination of who buys and sells what. When the prices are high, goods and services are not widely used, and when prices are low the opposite is true.

In terms of the theory of archetypes, prices are analogous to the human mind. Just as the mind controls the body and makes judgments about what the body should do, so prices control the economic system and the direction of sales and purchases. In the words of Adam Smith, price "determines the prudence or imprudence of all purchases and sales, and thereby regulates almost the whole of business" of economic life.[11]

Third, with the coming of civilization, a diversity of occupations has meant a diversity of "wages." Wages influence the amount of money in circulation and, hence, the vitality of the economy. Wages are the driving force in the economy that provides money to purchase goods and services. Those purchases affect the overall supply and demand for goods and services, as well as the prices.

The body functions in a way similar to wage functioning in an economic system. Just as the body follows the directives of the mind, so wages follow the directives of price. Smith believed that prices were determined largely by the cost of labor, so there is a reciprocal relationship between wages and prices, just as there is between mind and body. The body is the driving force which responds to and provides feedback to the mind. Part of that feedback is in the form of appetites and desires of the body, as noted by Plato. In the economic context, wages are spent to reflect the appetites of consumers and their demands for certain goods and services.

The theory of archetypes, as applied to economics, says that prices, wages and regulation are analogous to mind, body and spirit. As far as we know, these economic concepts originated with the beginnings of civilization, although they may have existed in rudimentary form in the times of pre-civilization. They are ideas which developed from man's perception of himself. Since they developed long after mankind began to populate the earth, they may be said to have existed in the nature of things- in the conditions of mankind as he approached the time of civilization. Just as teleology posits there is a design in nature placed there by God, so God may have placed these economic designs in human society.

Economic theory also contains two other important concepts that derive either from man's ideas or the design in nature. They are the principles of supply and demand. Supply and demand are mentioned in the writings of the classical economists, but our contemporary understanding of them is relatively recent, coinciding with the development of macroeconomics. Macroeconomics "did not even exist in its modern form until 1935, when John Maynard Keynes published his revolutionary *General Theory of Employment, Interest and Money*."[12] Demand, supply and government regulation have theoretical underpinnings in the theory of archetypes. Therefore, the theory as applied to economics shows that man's conception of mind, body and spirit applies to multiple concepts. Whether that conceptualization is the result of a design in nature or man's thoughts, the reader may draw his own conclusions.

MIND AS PRICE AND DEMAND FUNCTIONING

The economic system is driven by prices. Prices determine the amount of goods and services which will be produced and how they will be distributed. Even in primitive cultures, prices influence the future direction of the economy. If money does not exist, small quantities of valuable goods are exchanged for larger quantities of less valuable goods, and those who can do so will produce more of the valuable goods in order to become wealthy. In more advanced cultures, price will be represented by money and the monetary value of goods and services will influence their future production.

Prices are a key concept in microeconomic theory. Adam Smith is generally considered the founder of that theory, which is deals with "the behavior of individual entities such as markets, firms, and households."[13] In *The Wealth of Nations*, Smith considered "how individual prices are set, studied the determination of the prices of land, labor and capital, and inquired into the strengths and weaknesses of the market mechanism."[14]

Smith distinguished between two types of prices- the price of monopoly and the price of free competition. Obviously the latter was more desirable. The price of monopoly was the highest price that the monopolist could get in the marketplace. Smith believed that monopolists used the clever strategy of keeping the market continually understocked, so that they could charge a high price for their products. These prices were much higher than they would be under free competition.

In contrast the price of free competition, what Smith called the natural price, was the lowest possible price which sellers could take. This price was set by the requirements of sellers in order to "continue in their business."[15] In other words, free competition ensured that the lowest possible price was charged, while allowing businesses to make modest profits.

Smith believed that prices were determined primarily by the cost of labor, usually the largest expenditure in a business. He wrote that labor "is the only universal, as well as the only accurate measure of value, or the only standard by which we can compare the values of different commodities at all times and at all places."[16] Other classical economists agreed with Smith's ideas about labor. David Ricardo, for example, wrote that the price under free competition was associated with a natural price of labor itself. He noted that the natural price of labor was that which the laborer required to support himself and his family. The price of labor, therefore, depended on "the price of the food, necessaries, and conveniencies required for the support of the labourer and his family."[17]

Smith and the classical economists believed that prices were set, more or less rationally, by individual choices that collectively influenced the economic system. Today, price economists recognize the complex nature of how prices are determined. Smith's analysis of price determination was not based on "careful case studies of how businessmen actually do set prices, but on how they would set prices under assumed situations if they were motivated by rational considerations."[18] Contemporary economists are influenced by the work of John Maynard Keynes and others who have recognized the relationship between micro- and macro-economics in the determination of price levels.

Keynes believed that the general price level "depends partly on the wage-unit and partly on the volume of employment."[19] The cost of labor remains a major component for Keynes, as with the classical economists, but price also is influenced by employment. In his major work, *The General Theory of Employment, Interest, and Money*, Keynes argues that employment must be sustained in order for prices to remain fair and reasonable. During periods of economic downturn, it may be necessary for government to step in to maintain the proper level of employment for the overall health of the economy.

Although price is viewed as a more complex concept today, it still is analogous to the mind in the theory of archetypes. Price is no longer considered a purely rational mechanism, as it was for the classical economists, but it has certain non-rational and unpredictable elements. Price may be influenced by larger macro-economic forces, which in turn may be influenced by factors like the mood of investors and the direction of the stock market.

Mind has both rational and emotional elements, and so price is determined by both rational and non-rational means. While Smith emphasized the rational elements, Keynes and others emphasized the non-rational side of price determination. Keynes believed that in the long-run prices would behave rationally, but in the short-run they may not. In the short-run it may be necessary to simulate demand by government spending or tax cuts to put the price mechanism right again. He noted that manipulation of supply and demand was sometimes necessary to raise prices and wages to the proper level. Just as the emotions stimulate the mind to action, so active intervention into the macroeconomic system may be necessary from time to time to correct short-run problems in the microeconomic system.

Price is like the mind in a microeconomic system because it directs the activities of that system. It has rational and emotive power to direct when production should occur and on what level. But what about the macroeconomic level, where supply and demand are in operation? Does the theory of archetypes apply to the macroeconomic level? To answer that question, one must look for an initiating and directive force which operates like the mind. Among the three major macroeconomic forces- supply, demand and regulation- demand seems to fit that description best.

Smith notes that an increase in demand "though in the beginning it may sometimes raise the price of goods, never fails to lower it in the long run. It encourages production."[20] Demand is the driving and directing force that encourages production. It rationally allocates goods and resources to maximize production and lower price. Smith even believed that demand affected human populations. He wrote "the demand for men, like that of any other commodity, necessarily regulates the production of men…It is this demand which regulates and determines the state of propagation in all the different countries of the world."[21] Despite Smith's economic determinism, he makes one point clear. Demand is the initiating and directive force in economic affairs, much as the human mind is the initiating and directive force in human affairs.

Keynes also believed that demand was the directive force in economic prosperity. He argued that a "slump was simply a short-run problem stemming from a lack of demand. If the private sector was not prepared to spend to boost demand, the government should instead."[22] For Keynes, demand had both rational and irrational sides. It had the power to create unemployment and human suffering on a tremendous scale.

Like the human mind, demand is often complex and difficult to understand. What causes people to act in certain ways? Often there are complex motives at work. Similarly, demand in the economy may be the result of complex factors. As Samuelson and Nordhaus write:

> What determines the market demand for cornflakes or gasoline or computers? A whole array of factors influences how much will be demanded at a given price: average levels of income, the size of the population, the prices and availability of related goods, individual and social tastes, and special influences.[23]

Demand is best understood when it is viewed as an extension of the human mind. The mind directs the activities of the body, but it also responds to the requirements of the body. Similarly, demand for economic goods cannot be fully understood until it is viewed as responding to supply. Keynes noted this relationship in his discussion of classical economics. He wrote, the classical doctrine that "Supply creates its own demand" is still the basis of "all orthodox economic theory," but that this involves "a special assumption as to the relationship between these two functions."[24] Keynes differs from the classical economists in his description of that relationship, but still acknowledges the special influence of supply over demand.

Demand also is influenced by government regulation. Just as the mind is influenced by the spirit and given moral direction, so demand is influenced by government regulation to create an economy that benefits all citizens. Keynes wrote that the State "will have to exercise a guiding influence on the propensity to consume"[25] through its powers of taxation and regulation of the rate of interest. Thus, demand is held in check and given the proper direction by occasional government intervention.

Body as Wage and Supply Functioning

The body functions in a way similar to wage functioning in an economic system. Just as the body follows the directives of the mind, so wages follow the directives of price. Smith believed that prices were determined largely by the cost of labor, so there is a reciprocal relationship between wages and prices, just as there is between mind and body.

Smith wrote that the "whole annual produce of the land and labour of every country…naturally divides itself into three parts; the rent of the land, the wages of labour, and the profits of stock."[26] The wages of labor were a major component in the economy, and were greatly influenced by how much the capitalist could afford to pay his workers. In negotiating the price of labor, the "workmen desire to get as much as possible, the masters to give as little as possible."[27] So, wages were always a bone of contention between workers and capitalists, and always influenced by the prices which goods and services could fetch in the marketplace.

But wages are not determined solely by prices. Contemporary economists demonstrate that real wages, i.e. money wages divided by the cost of living, are determined by several factors related to the supply and demand of labor in a particular nation. Real wages may differ among nations because of factors such as lack of capital and lower education, which make marginal productivity lower in certain economies.[28]

The culture of particular nations also influences wages and economic productivity. Max Weber pointed out that a "man does not 'by nature' wish to earn more and more money, but simply to live as he is accustomed to live and to earn as much as is necessary for that purpose."[29] In *The Protestant Ethic and the Spirit of Capitalism*, Weber notes a stubborn resistance to work simply for the sake of becoming rich, but a culture imbued with the spirit of capitalism is more likely to motivate people to work for this end. In the United States, we have been guided by the spirit of capitalism from the beginning. Ben Franklin advocated the virtues of hard work in his writings, but Weber observes that Franklin's values were very lacking in moral virtue from the perspective pre-capitalist societies. According to Weber, Franklin's writings "would both in ancient times and in the Middle Ages have been proscribed as the lowest sort of avarice and an attitude entirely lacking in self-respect."[30]

Nevertheless, in modern times, wages are a driving force in the economy, providing money to purchase goods and services. Those purchases affect the overall supply and demand for goods and services, as well as price. The theory of archetypes says that the body is a driving force that responds to and provides feedback to the mind. Part of that feedback is in the form of the appetites and desires of the body, as Plato noted. In the economic context, wages are spent to reflect the appetites of consumers and their demands for certain goods and services.

Sometimes the appetites of the body (feedback influencing demand) are not good for its well-being in the long run. In economic terms, a lack of demand for certain goods and services may create a recession in the short run, or excessive demand may cause inflation for a brief time. But eventually, in the long run the body will right itself and yield to the intelligent directives of the mind. Keynes believed that an economic slump was a "short-run problem stemming from a lack of demand".[31] In The *General Theory*, he noted that "whatever happens to money-wages and prices in short runs, people confidently expect something close to long-run price stability."[32] The response to this problem should be to balance the budget in the medium term, but not in the short-run. To do otherwise would contribute to the problem by increasing unemployment and further lowering demand.

Keynes believed that the contemporary theory of unemployment during his time was "nonsense." In a depression, there is "no wage so low that it could eliminate unemployment," so it is "wicked to blame the unemployed for their plight".[33] For Keynes, the solution was government spending or reduced taxation to stimulate demand and overcome depression or recession. Just as the body needs intelligent interventions from the mind and spirit to correct short-term indiscretions, so the economy needs timely interventions from government to maintain stability and growth.

At the macroeconomic level, the body is an archetype for supply functions. Just as the body supplies physical force to meet the needs of the mind and spirit, so supply uses production to meet needs of the economy. Production is not an end in itself, rather it is a response to demand or consumption.

Smith pointed this out in *The Wealth of Nations*. He wrote, the "mercantile system absurdly considers production and not consumption to be the end of industry and commerce."[34] In his successful critique of the mercantilist system,

Smith observed "Restraints on importation of competing commodities sacrifice the interest of the consumer to the producer, and so do bounties on exportation."[35] Supply and production must serve demand and consumption in a successful economic system.

In the 20th century, Keynes observed that supply has a major effect on price and the overall health of the economic system. Prices "are governed by the conditions of supply and demand; and, in particular, changes in marginal cost and the elasticity of short-period supply".[36] If supply is inelastic in the short term, it can mean major increases in prices and significant problems for the economy. Therefore, supply elasticity is an important stabilizing force in the economy, particularly where vital industries are concerned.

Contemporary economists point out the complexity of factors affecting supply. A major element in determining supply is the cost of production. Production costs are determined by a range of factors such as the prices of inputs (e.g. labor, energy, machinery), by technological advances, by the prices of related goods, by governmental policy, and by special influences such as the weather.[37] Production costs sometimes make it difficult to predict that an adequate supply of goods and services will be available in the future.

In sum, supply responds to demand in the best economies, just as the body responds to the mind and spirit. The elasticity (flexibility) of supply in the short-term affects price and the overall economy, even as the body's flexibility and quickness in response to the demands of the mind and spirit ensure individual well-being. And, the complexity of production costs and the difficulty of predicting the short-term adequacy of supply are much like the complexities of the body and whether it can adequately meet the demands of the mind and spirit. Sometimes the spirit is willing but the flesh is weak.

The body is an archetype for supply in the macroeconomic system, and as such further analogies can be drawn. These limited points are meant to be merely illustrations. Time will tell how useful the theory of archetypes will be in predicting economic behavior.

Spirit as Taxation and Regulatory Functioning

Taxation is older than civilization itself. In aboriginal Hawaii, chiefdoms redistributed goods among the population even before there was a monied economy. The goods were used to support elites, maintain political relationships, and invest in economic projects like irrigation. In short, "redistributional mobilization was a form of taxation."[38]

The theory of archetypes recognizes the spirit as an archetype for taxation and regulatory functioning in an economic system. The spirit regulates the actions of the mind and body, supplying the moral values for their direction and resolving conflicts between the two. Similarly, taxation and government regulation influence the functioning of prices and wages, moderating their harshness for certain individuals and introducing principles of equity and justice into their operation.

Taxes redistribute wealth while, at the same time, serve a number of public purposes. Perhaps the most important purpose is the protection of lives and property from outside hostile forces. Government defends its citizens against war and invasion by an enemy, and thereby promotes security and economic prosperity.

Government regulation also serves useful and moral purposes by ensuring that business competition is fair and beneficial to society as a whole. Without any government regulation of industry, monopolies would form, competition would be stifled, and citizens would be vulnerable to unethical business practices. Therefore, taxation and regulation act as moderating influences, protecting society from harm both internally and externally.

Adam Smith recognized that government was indispensable. He believed it to be necessary for the security of private property and for a regular administration of justice, "to cause manufactures and commerce to flourish".[39] But sometimes taxation and regulation can become excessive, and inhibit proper functioning of the economic system. Smith warned against such action, in observing that taxes should take as little as possible from the people, because kings and ministers tend to be "the greatest spendthrifts in society".[40] Similarly, David Ricardo warned against excessive taxes on capital, because "they impair the funds for the maintenance of labor, and thereby diminish the future production of the country".[41]

In the 20th century, Keynesian economics had a more position view of taxation and regulation. Obviously, economic regulation was a necessary component of macroeconomic theory. On the subject of taxation, Keynes wrote that the state "will have to exercise a guiding influence on the propensity to consume partly through its scheme of taxation".[42] He noted, "Since the end of the nineteenth century significant progress toward the removal of very great disparities of wealth and income has been achieved through the instrument of taxation"[43] And, "I believe that there is social and psychological justification for significant inequalities of incomes and wealth, but not for such large disparities as exist today."[44]

For Keynes, taxation had a moral side as well as a practical economic side. Government was a moral agent, ensuring a more just distribution of income. This harks back to medieval times, where the Christian church exerted a great deal of influence on the state and also in the regulation of economic activity. As noted earlier, the idea of a "just wage and fair price"[45] was the cornerstone of the church's economic doctrine in the Middle Ages.

Today, the state has the same spiritual mandate that the church formerly had, and is the dominant moral force in the regulation of business activities. That mandate applies moral principles to regulation and taxation, based on the idea that moderation often brings the most justice to all parties. As mind and body should be in balance, so should the proper regulation of economic activities.

But, just as the spirit can exert excessive influence over the mind and body, so government taxation and regulation can be excessive, creating economic problems. Samuelson and Nordhaus note that for the past two decades, "many economists have argued that most economic regulation was actually creating monopoly power rather than curbing it."[46] They observe that most economic studies "suggest that the main effects of economic regulation are losses in efficiency and large amounts of income redistribution."[47]

Government should allow the economy to operate and do what it does best- to use the law of supply and demand to provide goods and services at the lowest price. Yet, government needs to step in when the marketplace does not provide for the needs of its citizenry. The spirit must know when to intervene and how often its help is needed.

CONCLUSIONS

In this chapter, the theory of archetypes has been applied to micro and macro-economic principles. Table 3 summarizes the essential elements. Often, these principles are inseparable in practice. When prices are not guided by the regulatory principles of justice and productivity, various forms of economic corruption may result, e.g. monopolies, price fixing, and unfair competition. On the other hand, when regulation and government control is oppressive, prices and wages are not fairly determined by the market and individual productivity. Just as the spirit cannot impose unrealistic restrictions on the mind or body, so government cannot impose undue restrictions on the freedom of prices and wages to determine their proper levels.

Table 3. Economics and the Theory of Archetypes

Micro-Economics
Mind/Prices
Prices are like the mind, because they direct the actions of the economic system. They determine the amount of goods and services that will be produced and how they will be distributed.
Body/Wages
Wages are like the body, because they are the physical entity in the economy that allows the purchase of goods and services. Wages respond to the direction of prices, but also influence prices themselves.
Spirit/Taxes
Taxes are like the spirit, because they apply the principles of fairness and equity to the economic system. Taxes redistribute wealth and provide for common services necessary to the existence of a moral and ethical society.
Macro-Economics
Mind/Demand
Demand is like the mind, because it is a directive force in the economy. It rationally allocates goods and services to maximize production and lower price, and it is a directive force in economic prosperity.
Body/Supply
Supply is like the body, because it responds to the directives of demand and physically supplies goods and services needed by the economy. It also supplies input to the forces of demand and modifies their actions.
Spirit/Regulation
Regulation is like the spirit, because it provides for just and fair practices in the economic system. Regulation should ensure moral and ethical practices by businesses, while avoiding undue interference with the laws of supply and demand.

In the economic sphere, regulation should encourage justice, productivity and innovation. It sets the tone for prices, which in turn determine fairness in wages. If prices are not determined according to the principles of fairness, then dysfunctions in the system occur. Similarly, if wages are not determined from prices, human suffering results.

Apart from a general understanding, the theory of archetypes also should be applied to address perennial problems in economics. One such problem is the need to avoid recession, where prices and wages rise too slowly, or even fall to dangerous levels. If the trigger for recession is a slump in prices (related to mind), it may be similar to a lapse or a period of depression in the human health context. Healthy mental activity may be restored simply by vigilance and the proper attitude, or it may require a chemical intervention if more serious. Changing chemical reactions in the body may be related to altering wages, since the theory of archetypes posits a relationship between the body and wage functioning. Hypotheses of these sorts could be tested after the development of a more thorough understanding of the application of the theory to economics.

Similarly, inflation might be viewed as a condition where the mind is overly stimulated. Inflation occurs when prices and wages rise too quickly, and in the human health context, anxiety is a condition where the mind is overly stimulated. Once again, the cure for this condition may be through behavioral intervention, trying to reduce anxious thoughts and the stimuli that produce them. Or, the condition may require chemical intervention, where the body is able to help the mind reduce anxiety through altering its chemistry. The choice between the two often depends on the severity of the condition and the ability of the mind to aid itself without help from the body.

Economics is a field of knowledge where concepts are highly interrelated, where prices affect wages, wages affect prices, taxes affect prices, etc. It also is a field where the results of theory can be assessed very quickly. If a particular approach does not work, it becomes readily apparent in the economic result. The greatest difficulty is untangling the concepts to determine why it has not worked. The theory of archetypes may aid in that process, because all concepts are derived from mind, body and spirit and their interrelationships.

NOTES

[1] George Dalton. "Aboriginal Economies in Stateless Societies," in *Exchange Systems in Prehistory*. Timothy K. Earle and Jonathon E. Ericson (Eds). (New York: Academic Press, 1977), 191.
[2] Ibid., 203.
[3] George Soule. *Ideas of the Great Economists*. (New York: Mentor Books, 1952), 8.
[4] Ibid., 9.
[5] Ibid., 9.
[6] Ibid., 10.
[7] Ibid., 11.
[8] Ibid., 11.
[9] Ibid., 12.
[10] Ibid., 16.
[11] Adam Smith, "From Adam Smith," *in Man & The State: The Political Philosophers*. Saxe Commins and Robert Linscott (Eds.).(New York: Washington Square Press, 1966), 348.
[12] Paul Samuelson and William Nordhaus *Economics*, 16th Edition. (Boston: McGraw Hill, 1998), 5.
[13] Ibid., 5.
[14] Ibid., 5.

[15] Adam Smith. *The Wealth of Nations*. (New York: Modern Library, 1937), 219.
[16] Smith, in Commins and Linscott, op. cit., 346.
[17] David Ricardo. from Principles of Economy and Taxation (1817), in *Masterworks of Economics*. Leonard Abbott (Ed.). (Garden City, NY: Doubleday, 1946), 310.
[18] Soule, op. cit., 106.
[19] John Maynard Keynes. *The General Theory of Employment, Interest, and Money*. (New York: Harcourt Brace Jovanovich, Publishers, 1953), 295.
[20] Smith, op. cit.,706.
[21] Ibid., 80.
[22] http://bized.ac.uk/virtual/economy/library/economists/keynesth/htm.
[23] Samuelson & Nordhaus, op. cit., 46.
[24] Keynes, op. cit., 25.
[25] Ibid., 378.
[26] Smith, op. cit., Book 1, Chapter 6.
[27] Smith, in Commins and Linscott, op. cit., 381.
[28] Samuelson & Nordhaus, op. cit., 228.
[29] Max Weber. *The Protestant Ethic and the Spirit of Capitalism*. (New York" Charles Scribner's Sons, 1958), 60.
[30] Ibid., 56.
[31] http://bized, op. cit.
[32] James Tobin. "An Overview of the General Theory." *A 'Second Edition' of the General Theory*. G.C. Harcourt and P.A. Riach (Eds.). (London: Routledge, 1997), 25.
[33] www_groups.dcs.st-and.ac.uk/~history/mathematicians/keynes.html.
[34] Smith, op. cit., 625.
[35] Ibid, 625.
[36] Keynes, op. cit., 292.
[37] Samuelson and Nordhaus, op. cit., 49.
[38] Dalton, op. cit., 226.
[39] Smith, op. cit., 862.
[40] Ibid., Book 2, Chapter 11.
[41] Ricardo, op. cit., 335.
[42] Keynes, op. cit., 378.
[43] Ibid., 372
[44] Ibid., 374.
[45] Soule, op. cit., 12.
[46] Samuelson & Nordhaus, op. cit., 309.
[47] Ibid., 309.

Chapter 4

PSYCHOLOGY

In the twentieth century, the field of psychology was influenced by a number of forces, but one of the greatest of these was Sigmund Freud. Freud's work was particularly influential in the first part of the century, following the publication of *The Interpretation of Dreams* and subsequent works. One of his key concepts was the division of the human personality into three elements: the id, ego and superego. These concepts provide almost a perfect fit to the theory of archetypes.

The id involves basic instincts, so naturally it is like the body. The ego receives sensations from the body and controls the impulses of the id, and therefore is like the mind. The superego is the conscience, controlling the impulses of the id at the unconscious level; therefore it is like the spirit, which consists of conscience, values and ethics. In this chapter, Freud's theory of personality will be linked to the theory of archetypes in some detail.

Another theory of major import in the twentieth century was behaviorism. Behaviorism began with the writings of John Watson, and developed in the twentieth century with the work of B.F. Skinner. Instrumental or operant conditioning begins with a plan of reinforcement to induce certain behaviors through stimulus and response. The plan of reinforcement is analogous to the spirit, because it supplies the principles and goals for which the new behavior is created. Stimulus is like the mind directing the body to do something- the more powerful the stimulus the more powerful the reaction of the body. And, of course, the body is like the response, and guiding its course of action is the whole purpose of the exercise. The response may be unpredictable at times, but generally it follows the pattern of the stimulus. This chapter will apply the theory of archetypes to behaviorism and explain these important concepts.

Freud's Theory of Personality

In his seminal work, *The Interpretation of Dreams*, Freud wrote that all dreams are egotistical. Whenever "my ego does not appear in the context of the dream" it "lies in another person."[1] These other persons might be family, friends, strangers, or enemies, but usually they are symbolic of something with deeper meaning.

Typically dreams also include primal forces in the mind, which Freud called the libido or id, that are at war with the ego. In discussing the symbolism of dreams, Freud wrote, "It might be said that the wild beasts are used to represent the libido, a force dreaded by the ego and combated by means of repression."[2] The ego represses the basic instincts of the libido, sometimes to the benefit of the psyche, and sometimes not. When repression becomes too strong it harmfully diverts the libido "from its purpose" and the libido finds "no employment."[3] This may result in a pathology known as "neurotic anxiety".[4]

The Id and the Body

In his later writings, Freud defined the id as containing "everything that is inherited, that is present at birth, that is laid down in the constitution- above all, therefore, the instincts."[5] Writers who followed Freud summarized his concept of the id as "a sort of storehouse of motives and 'instinctual' reactions for satisfying motives. These motives taken together, are called the *libido*."[6] So, the id consists of the libido and the instinctual reactions for satisfying it.

The id also is described in relation to the pursuit of pleasure. The pleasure principle "is what dominates the id."[7] The id seeks pleasure for the body, while "the main task of the ego is to moderate the id's pursuit of pleasure."[8] In the struggle between the ego and the id, compromise "is unknown to the unconscious instinctual id".[9] The id represents the strong, primal desires of the body to seek comfort and pleasure.

It is not difficult to see how the id and the body are similar, if not identical, in the theory of archetypes. In fact, Freud's theory of personality seems to confirm the importance of mind, body and spirit in the development of man's thinking. The id comes from man's body- its physical strength and its desire for pleasure. Its effect on personality is important for Freud, in that its desires must be understood and respected if man is to be healthy psychologically. And yet, it must be controlled by the mind or ego in order for its expression to be acceptable in society. Freud believed that the ego should control the id, just as the theory of archetypes says the mind should control the body.

The Ego and the Mind

In his *Outline of Psychoanalysis*, Freud writes that the ego "acts as an intermediary between the id and the external world."[10] It performs that task "by gaining control over the demands of the instincts."[11] The ego acts as a "logical force"[12] which governs the irrational demands of the id. In addition, the ego has "the task of self-preservation." Responding to external events, the ego becomes "aware of stimuli, by storing up experiences about them (in the memory)".[13] The ego acts exactly like the mind in its control of the body, and its processing of information for storage in the memory.

However, the ego is not exactly like the mind in every way. Freud believed that the ego represented rational thought and logic. The capacity to think logically "is above all an attribute of the ego."[14] In order for an individual to reach human maturity, the ego has to become "master of its own house".[15] But passions were associated with the id, rather than the ego. The ego "is the conscious self representing 'what may be called reason and common sense, in contrast to the id, which contains the passions."[16] Freud believed that logic and reason were needed to maintain a tight reign on passions, just as the ego needed to maintain supremacy over the id. Human emotions were viewed negatively compared to the views of contemporary psychology.

Today, psychology recognizes that emotions are an important aspect of the mind, and often work in harmony with the mind's faculties of reason and logic. But for Freud, the ego was passionless. The ego consisted of "elaborate ways of behaving and thinking that are learned for dealing effectively with the world. It delays the satisfaction of motives or channels motives into social acceptable outlets."[17] So, in combination with the id, the ego produced reason and allowed passion to be expressed in socially acceptable ways. The ego was the master, and the id was the driving force that pursued pleasure.

In terms of the theory of archetypes, the mind is clearly an archetype for the ego, at least, that aspect of the mind involving logic, reason, memory and other higher functions. Just as the theory of archetypes posits that the mind should direct the body, so Freud believed that the ego should direct the id. And as the theory of archetypes acknowledges the important of feedback from the body in directing the mind, so Freud believed that the ego should not so dominate the id that the id finds self-expression in harmful ways.

Freud believed that the process needed to be governed by the superego, which provides moral direction and guidance for the ego. The theory of archetypes also posits the need for a third force- the spirit- in guiding and directing the mind. The spirit and the superego share a number of common traits.

The Superego and the Spirit

The superego corresponds with what is commonly called conscience. It "consists of restraints, acquired in the course of personality development, on the activity of the ego and the id."[18] While the ego controls the id, the superego controls them both. The ego needs control because the intellect may find itself in a moral quandary, where logic and reason are not sufficient in solving a problem or dealing with a situation. The superego is "the force of conscience"[19] which has the power to enforce itself on the ego when moral values are needed.

In the words of Freud, the superego is a "special agency" in which "parental influence is prolonged."[20] Parents and other authority figures, like teachers, influence the development of the superego in children. Parents are especially influential, as Freud believed that the complex interactions between the ego and superego "become completely intelligible when they are traced back to the child's attitude to its parents."[21]

When children misbehave, they are punished. Memories of that punishment persist into adulthood in the form of dreams, according to Freud. The relations between the ego and superego can be more clearly understood by studying dreams, by analyzing the actions of the superego and its development. Freud wrote, "Since psychoanalysis has divided the personality into an ego and super-ego…it has become easy to recognize in these punishment dreams fulfillments of the wishes of the super-ego."[22]

The superego has both positive and negative sides to its operation. The positive side is that individuals are taught to behave in ways that are moral, according to the values of parents and other authority figures. If those values are good, then the behavior is good. But the negative side is that the superego may become overly developed and overly critical of the ego. The superego "judges, condemns, rewards, and punishes," which if carried to extremes explains why "certain persons suffer from an overly severe conscience."[23] Freud himself was driven to "constant work by a harsh superego."[24] According to one scholar, he suffered from a "ruthless suppression of his longings for love and pleasure."[25]

The theory of archetypes states that the spirit should control the mind, but that its control should not be excessive. The mind should be allowed to do its work, with intervention from the spirit only on occasions when decisions require moral and ethical input. Similarly, the superego's input should not be excessive or it distorts the proper activities of the ego. The parallel between Freud's theory and the theory of archetypes is very strong in that respect.

But the parallel is less strong in describing the nature and origin of the superego versus the spirit. The superego, like the spirit, provides moral and ethical guidelines which shape the individual, but it originates in parental authority and the values of authority figures. Freud was an atheist, so it makes sense that his moral values did not come from the spirit, which normally is associated with God. Thus, the origins of values in Freud's superego and spirit are quite different.

The Theories of Behaviorism

Behaviorism began with John Watson's seminal work, entitled *Behaviorism*. In that book, Watson proposed that psychology should study human learning and behavior by understanding the concepts of stimulus and response. The laboratory experiments of Pavlov were influential in developing this new approach to psychology.

As behaviorism began to grow in influence, new theories developed. B.F. Skinner's theory of operant conditioning emphasized the importance of reinforcement on learning and the interactions of stimulus and response. By the mid-twentieth century, behaviorism expanded in influence beyond psychology to other social sciences. In political science, for example, behaviorism in the 1950s focused on the explanation and prediction of legislative and voter behavior.

The fundamental concepts of behaviorism are stimulus, response and reinforcement. In the theory of archetypes, they are related to mind, body and spirit. The reminder of this chapter is devoted to discussing that relationship.

Stimulus and the Mind

Watson founded the school of behaviorism based on his understanding of stimulus and response. In his words, "behavioristic psychology has as its goal to be able, given the stimulus, to predict the response- or, seeing the reaction take place to state what the stimulus is that has called out the reaction."[26]

It all begins with a stimulus, which causes a response to occur in the organism. Watson believed that stimuli could be either external or internal, coming from either outside or inside of the organism. Stimuli were a constant influence on the body. He wrote, "the organism is constantly assailed by stimuli-which come through the eye, the ear, the nose and the mouth- the so-called objects of our environment; at the same time the inside of our body is likewise assailed at every moment by stimuli arising from changes in the tissues themselves."[27]

A stimulus causes something to happen, and is an initiating force. The behaviorists believed that the body itself could be a stimulus, influencing the mind to respond in a particular way. Or, the mind could be affected, through the senses, by outside forces. It would appear, in terms of the theory of archetypes, that stimuli would be more related to the body than the mind, since the body initiates many stimuli. But, it must be remembered that the theory of archetypes says that the mind is the initiating force, causing the body to respond in particular ways. In assessing stimulus and response, it is clear that stimulus is the initiating force and response is the responder to that force. Therefore, stimulus is like the mind in its operation, according to the theory of archetypes.

In psychology, stimuli are studied in different ways. Behavioralists "focus on the physical qualities of the stimulus (e.g. the sound vibrations of the bell)."[28] Gestalt and phenomenological theorists treat the stimulus "as a complex phenomenon, including meaning as well as physical attributes".[29] And, experimental psychologists use research design to isolate and study important stimuli related to human behavior. They "try to maximize the control of behavior by excluding almost all stimuli except the focal stimulus."[30]

The stimulus is like the mind in its complexity. We use stimuli every day to influence the world around us. For example, B.F. Skinner notes that we use stimuli "to eliminate behavior [that we don't like] by evoking incompatible responses."[31] Citing an actual case study, Skinner writes: "When women employed in a factory created a hazard by hurrying down a corridor at the end of the day, the manager put up mirrors along the corridor to evoke responses of adjusting wearing apparel and applying cosmetics."[32]

Skinner also notes that we use stimuli regularly in our daily interactions with other people. We use "supplemental stimuli" when we try to encourage others to "interpret a situation favorably".[33] For example, this occurs "when the salesman assures the potential buyer that he will enjoy or profit from a purchase, or when we encourage someone to join us on a given occasion by assuring him of enjoyable consequences."[34]

The stimulus is like the mind in that it is an initiating force, and that it is complex in its operations and motives. The power of the mind over the body is best understood when viewed as a symbiotic relationship, a relationship of mutual benefit. Similarly, the operations of the stimulus are best understood when viewed in relationship to its counterpart, the response.

Response and the Body

The father of behaviorism, John Watson, linked stimulus and response in the following way- "the organism does something when it is assailed by stimuli. It responds. It moves."[35] He goes on to describe the response: "usually the response that the organism makes to the stimulus brings about an adjustment, though not always. By an adjustment we mean merely that the organism by moving so alters its physiological state that the stimulus no longer arouses reaction."[36] The response is an adjustment that keeps the stimulus from bothering the organism further.

Watson also believed that responses, like stimuli, could be either internal or external. Internal responses occur inside the body, such as chemical responses brought about by chemical stimuli, or alterations in thought produced by other ideas. External responses are more easily observed, as they are manifest in the form of actual behavior. For instance, the light shines in someone's eyes, so they move to avoid the direct glare from a window.

The early behavioralists did not define and study the response as carefully as they did the stimulus. Watson and others "were content to say that connections were formed between stimulus and response"[37] and leave it at that. Their major focus was on understanding the stimulus and its impact on the response. But as behaviorialism developed, more attention was devoted to understanding the response, and how it affected the stimulus.

C.L. Hull and later behavioralists began to look at the influence of intervening variables on stimulus and response. Hull believed the connection between stimulus and response "could accumulate units of *habit strength* through repetition and reinforcement."[38] Thus, reinforcement became an important variable and a major determinant of habit strength.

Skinner thought responses should be divided into two categories- Type S and Type R. He proposed that "automatic reflexes like the salivary reflex be called Type S, and responses emitted by the organism in the absence of an identifiable external stimulus be called Type R."[39] Skinner called the Type R response "an 'operant' because it operated on the environment."[40] Operant conditioning became the cornerstone of his theory of behaviorism.

Skinner wrote that it is "customary to refer to any movement of the organism as a 'response.' The word is borrowed from the field of reflex action and implies an act which, so to speak, answers a prior event- the stimulus. But one may make an event contingent upon behavior without identifying, or being able to identify, a prior stimulus."[41] In other words, in classical conditioning "a reinforcer is paired with a stimulus"[42]- food (reinforcement) is given to a dog after a bell is rung which announces mealtime (stimulus). But in operant conditioning, the "operant behavior is contingent upon a response"[43]- a pigeon pecks a tab a certain number of times (response) before it is given food (reinforcement).

The response is like the body in the theory of archetypes for several reasons. First, the body responds to the direction of the mind in the same way that the response automatically responds to the stimulus (in Type S responses). Second, the body can influence the mind and spirit by its actions in the same way that response, through habit strength or operant conditioning, can influence stimulus and reinforcement. Third, and perhaps speculatively, the body operates best when it cooperates with the mind and spirit in a subordinate role; in the same way responses are most productive when they are appropriate to the level of stimulus and the degree of reinforcement. When they exceed those factors, the organism suffers from lack of adaptability.

Reinforcement and the Spirit

In the early writings of behaviorism, reinforcement was not emphasized. In fact, the word "reinforcement" is not even found in the index of Watson's landmark book *Behaviorism*. Perhaps the closest he comes to mentioning it is in the phrase, "Training enlarges the range of stimuli."[44] Watson and the early behaviorists focused on stimulus and response, and parenthetically mentioned training as a way or reinforcing a response.

Skinner's emphasis on schedules of reinforcement began "in an off-handed way."[45] Once he found himself short of food pellets for reinforcement, so he began reinforcing only occasional responses. He found that intermittent reinforcement was more effective in maintaining response than regular reinforcement.[46] Skinner concluded that the "net result of reinforcement is not simply to strengthen behavior but to strengthen it in a given state of deprivation. Reinforcement thus brings behavior under the control of an appropriate deprivation. After we have conditioned a pigeon to stretch its neck by reinforcing with food, the variable which controls neck-stretching is food deprivation."[47]

So, reinforcement requires deprivation of some kind to be effective in most cases. Another thing that Skinner observed was that reinforcement is most effective when it involves some sort of delay. He discovered the delay in schedules of reinforcement made pigeons response more strongly. He wrote that many "social and commercial reinforcements are of this sort- where, for example, the net effect is reduced if one replies too quickly or agrees too readily to an arrangement or where an optimal reinforcement follows only after 'due deliberation.'"[48]

Negative reinforcers have much power in influencing animal behavior, but positive reinforcers also are important, especially in human behavior. Skinner writes that if "an individual produces money or goods, he may use them for purposes of reinforcement in the form of wages, bribes, or gratuities."[49] Thus, a wealthy man or woman may use money as a reinforcement to produce the proper response and to control behavior. In a similar way, "sexual simulation" is "a common form of reinforcement and is widely used in personal control."[50] Positive reinforcement can take many forms.

Skinner's theory of operant conditioning, or instrumental learning, differs from classical conditioning in several ways. First, the learner is "active and emits responses instead of having responses elicited from him."[51] A learner can choose to ignore the reinforcement or to give in to it- a response is not forced out of him. And second, in operant conditioning "reinforcement is contingent only upon certain responses."[52] The reinforcement does not occur automatically, but only when a learner responds in a certain way. It is used to direct the learner to the desired behavior.

Much of Skinner's research emphasized the use of positive reinforcers to elicit behavior. From his data, he inferred that "we reinforce not a response, but a class of responses"[53] and the word "operant" was used to describe this class. Operant conditioning emphasized the fact that "behavior operates on the environment to generate consequences."[54] In other words, reinforcement was used to shape a response in a particular environment. As an example, Skinner was able "to teach a pigeon to play Ping-Pong by reinforcing, first, any peck in the direction of the ball, later any peck striking the ball, then any peck knocking it in the desired direction."[55] For Skinner, shaping had a "marked similarity to the procedure parents use in teaching a small child a skill such as riding a two-wheel bike."[56] In the words of Skinner, reinforcing contingencies "shape the behavior of the individual, and novel contingencies generate novel forms of behavior."[57]

Reinforcement is a powerful tool that shapes behavior in everyday life. In the theory of archetypes, it operates like the spirit in providing the desired direction for activity. Just as the spirit guides the mind and body in their operations, so reinforcement guides stimulus and response to reach a desired outcome. The spirit provides needed moral direction for the mind and body, just as reinforcement shapes behavior by manipulating the appropriate stimulus and response.

However, there is one important difference between the spirit and reinforcement. The spirit intervenes only occasionally in the operations of the mind and body, allowing them to perform their activities normally without interference. But reinforcement is constantly at work in its influence on stimulus and response. Without reinforcement, higher levels of learning would not be possible. One might say that intermittent reinforcement schedules are analogous to the spirit's intermittent influence, but reinforcement must be there on a regular basis in order for behavior to be affected.

CONCLUSIONS

Table 4 summarizes the application of the theory of archetypes to psychology.

Table 4. Psychology and the Theory of Archetypes

Freud
Mind/Ego
The ego is like the mind, because it is a rational and directive force in the human personality. It uses reason, logic, memory and other higher functions to allow adaptation and self-preservation.
Body/Id
The id is like the body, because it is instinctual in nature and a powerful physical force in the human personality. The id seeks pleasure, but it also submits to the control of the ego.
Spirit/Superego
The superego is like the spirit, because it provides moral and ethical values in the form of a conscience. Conscience in the human personality is developed from the values of parents and authority figures.
Behaviorism
Mind/Stimulus
Stimulus is like the mind, because it initiates and directs the learning process. Like the mind, stimulus can be complex in its operations.
Body/Response
Response is like the body, because it responds to the direction of the stimulus. It is the physical force that demonstrates that learning has occurred.
Spirit/Reinforcement
Reinforcement is like the spirit, because it shapes behavior by applying certain principles or values. It guides stimulus and response with a plan for producing the desired behavior.

The development of psychology in the twentieth century owes a great deal to the theories of Freud and the behaviorists. The Freudian theory of personality, consisting of id, ego and superego, is almost an exact parallel to the theory of archetypes. The id is like the body, a powerful instinctual force that seeks pleasure, yet is subservient to the ego. The ego is like the mind, a major directive force in human activities, yet different from the mind in its lack of emotion and passion. The superego is like the spirit in its provision of moral and ethical direction to the ego and id, much as the spirit provides direction to the mind and body.

The parallel between Freud's theory and the theory of archetypes demonstrates that mind, body and spirit are essential to man's personality and to his thinking. The personality influences how we perceive the world and the categories of knowledge that we apply to it. Personality provides an imprint for our understanding of other phenomena.

Similarly, the essential elements of behaviorism- stimulus, response and reinforcement- have parallels in mind, body and spirit. Stimulus is like the mind in providing direction to the learning process. It controls the degree and nature of response from the body. Response itself is like the body, which responds to the direction and control of the mind. The response, like the body, is the most visible evidence that learning has occurred. And reinforcement is like the spirit in providing direction to the overall process of learning. Much of operant conditioning involves the use of varying schedules of reinforcement to influence stimulus and response. But, unlike the operations of the spirit in man, reinforcement is not used infrequently. It is an active participant in the process.

The theory of archetypes applies to behaviorism and has some potential for clarifying the relationships between stimulus, response and reinforcement. For example, the spirit's direction of the mind, on an infrequent basis to provide moral direction, might be applied more literally to the application of reinforcement to stimulus. We might pay more attention to the more limited and ethical use of reinforcement in human interaction. Reinforcement, like the spirit, might be used more judiciously and with more attention to moral considerations. Since it is a powerful force, it might be used with more care.

Notes

[1] Sigmund Freud. *The Interpretation of Dreams*. (New York: Avon Books, 1968), 358.
[2] Ibid., 445.
[3] Ibid., 195.
[4] Ibid., 195.
[5] Sigmund Freud. "Selection From: An Outline of Psychoanalysis. The Psychical Apparatus." *Readings for an Introduction to Psychology*. Richard A. King (Ed.). (New York: McGraw-Hill, 1971), 338.
[6] Clifford T. Morgan and Richard A. King. *Introduction to Psychology*. (New York: McGraw-Hill, 1966),490.
[7] C.R. Badcock. *The Psychoanalysis of Culture*. (Oxford: Basil Blackwell, 1980), 218.
[8] Ibid., 219.
[9] Ibid., 98.
[10] Freud, "Selection From…," op. cit., 338.
[11] Ibid., 339.
[12] Freud, *The Interpretation of Dreams*, op. cit., 88.
[13] Freud, "Selection From…," op. cit., 339.
[14] Badcock, op. cit., 98.
[15] Ibid., 231.
[16] Louis Breger. *Freud: Darkness in the Midst of Vision*. (New York: John Wiley & Sons, 2000), 272.
[17] Morgan and King, op. cit., 490.
[18] Ibid., 490.
[19] Badcock, op. cit., 5.
[20] Freud, "Selection From…," op. cit., 339.
[21] Ibid., 339.
[22] Freud, *The Interpretation of Dreams*, op. cit., 519.
[23] Breger, op. cit., 272.
[24] Ibid., 272.
[25] Ibid., 329.
[26] John B. Watson. *Behaviorism*. (New York: WW Norton, 1970), 18.
[27] Ibid., 12.
[28] Ross Stagner. *A History of Psychological Theories*. (New York: Collier MacMillan, 1988), 195.
[29] Ibid., 195.
[30] Ibid., 195.
[31] B.F.Skinner. *Science and Human Behavior*. (New York: The Free Press, 1965), 316.
[32] Ibid., 316.
[33] Ibid., 316.
[34] Ibid., 316.
[35] Watson, op. cit., 14.
[36] Ibid., 14.
[37] Stagner, op. cit., 202.
[38] Ibid., 203.
[39] Ibid., 222.
[40] Ibid., 223.
[41] Skinner, op. cit., 64.
[42] Ibid., 65.
[43] Ibid., 65.
[44] Watson, op. cit., 13.
[45] David Hothersall. *History of Psychology*. (Philadelphia: Temple University Press, 1984), 399.
[46] Ibid., 399.
[47] Skinner, op. cit., 149.

[48] Ibid., 126.
[49] Ibid., 317.
[50] Ibid., 317.
[51] Morgan and King, 88.
[52] Ibid., 88.
[53] Stagner, 224.
[54] Ibid., 22.
[55] Ibid., 223.
[56] Ibid., 223.
[57] Skinner, 255.

Chapter 5

SOCIOLOGY

The field of sociology is greatly influenced by the work of Auguste Comte and Emile Durkheim. Comte is widely considered to be "the father of sociology"[1] and Durkheim was the first scholar to apply Comte's theories to "an actual systematic study of society."[2] Together, their theories and research form the foundation of the modern discipline of sociology.

Both Comte and Durkheim developed theories that relate to the subject of this book- the theory of archetypes. Comte, in particular, was enamored of theories having three parts, and the foundation of his most famous theory is linked to the theory of archetypes. Durkheim's famous study on suicide also has a strong connection to the theory of archetypes, as well as his more general theories.

THE THEORIES OF COMTE

J.S. Mill wrote "Comte's 'most fundamental theory' was the idea of the three successive stages of thought from theological to metaphysical and finally to positive."[3] The theory proposes "three intellectual stages through which the world has gone throughout its history."[4] In the first stage, the theological stage, man sought knowledge of the activities of supernatural beings and their influence on civilization. This period began with early man and lasted until approximately 1300 A.D. During the second stage, the metaphysical, man believed that abstract forces in nature, rather than a God or gods, produced all phenomena. This period lasted from about 1300 to 1800 A.D. And the final period, the positive or scientific, began with man's belief in science as the source of knowledge. This period began in 1800 and continues into the present time.[5]

Although the theory of intellectual progress is Comte's major theory, it is merely part of a larger theoretical framework. Comte believed that "progress may be broken up into three constituent parts- intellectual, material and moral."[6] The parallel between this theory and the theory of archetypes is fairly clear. *Intellectual progress* is progress of the mind; *material progress* is the physical progress of man, physical referring to the body; and *moral progress* is related to morality and matters of the spirit.

As mentioned earlier, Comte had a great fondness for theories with three parts, some of which related directly to mind, body and spirit. His theories included "three stages of intellectual progress, three divisions of cerebral functions, three types of social forces, three grades of society, three social classes, three stages of religion, and three classes of regulating power in society."[7] But perhaps the theory with the strongest linkage to the theory of archetypes was the theory of cerebral functions.

Comte believed that "social evolution, like social organization, is a product of the tripartite functions of man's cerebral system- feeling, action and intellect."[8] He took his ideas about cerebral functioning from the Franz Gall's phrenology and made them "the basis of his psychology and much of his social science."[9] There are obvious parallels between feeling and the spirit, action and the body, and intellect and the mind.

Comte found that feeling or emotion was "the basis for morality"[10] in society. Feeling is less powerful than intellect, in Comte's estimation, but the two must be unified in order for a modern society to exist. In fact, their unity in a "Positive system" requires "the subordination of the intellect to the heart."[11] When the intellect is subordinate to the heart, there is a "synthesis of feelings" which directs the body to act, in a "synthesis of actions."[12] Thus mind is subordinate to feelings, and body is subordinate to the mind. This is precisely how it works in the theory of archetypes, if the spirit is understood as expressing itself through the heart.

The moral force in society is "based on affection and expressed in command prompted by character and obedience prompted by the heart."[14] Yet, the heart by itself is not enough to prompt obedience to social norms. Comte writes that self-love is a stronger force in man than social sympathy. Social instincts in man "would never gain the mastery were they not sustained and called into constant exercise by the economy of the external world".[15] The moral unity of man and of his society would not be possible without recognizing "our subjection to an external power."[16] For Comte, that power was society and the state. For others, it may be the power of God, the ultimate moral force.

The second element in the cerebral system is action. Man's "activational evolution proceeds through the stages of conquest, defense, and industry."[17]

Action is the material force in society by which man accomplishes his goals, much as the body accomplishes the directives of the intellect. Comte believed that there were three major forces in society-moral, material and intellectual. The material force, like the body, is a social force which first leads to conquest of enemies, then defense of territory, and finally to production and industry. Comte was fond of applying the cerebral functions to the evolution of human history.

The third cerebral element is the intellect. The parallel to the mind in the theory of archetypes is obvious. The evolution of the intellect follows Comte's famous three stages- theological, metaphysical, and positive or scientific. In this process, "emotion is the dynamic power, action the agent of progress, and the intellect the guiding force."[18] While the intellect is subordinate to feeling and emotion, it must organize itself first before the heart can take over. In Comte's words, "The truth is, and it is a truth of great importance, that Thoughts must be systematised before Feelings, Feelings before Actions."[19] The mind must be aware of a problem before the spirit and the body can respond.

It is clear that Comte's theories of cerebral functioning and social progress are related to the theory of archetypes. But what about his major theory- the three stages of intellectual progress? How do the theological, metaphysical and positive stages align with the mind, body and spirit?

In the theological stage, the human mind "supposes all phenomena to be produced by the immediate action of supernatural beings."[20] Spiritual explanations are used to explain natural phenomena, and man's belief in the supernatural guides all of his thinking. In terms of the theory of archetypes, the theological stage is a period of thinking dominated by the spirit. Spiritual power is the source of direction in the universe, and is the means by which man communicates with the supernatural powers.

In the metaphysical stage, man identifies abstract forces in nature as the powerful elements in his life. Both personified abstractions and actual entities produce all phenomena. Like the mind in the theory of archetypes, the metaphysical stage relies on abstractions to explain the natural world. The essence of the mind is abstraction, and abstractions are used to explain the world in the metaphysical stage.

In the positive or scientific stage, "the mind gives up the vain search for absolute notions, the origin and destination of the universe, and the causes of phenomena, and studies their laws".[21] The positive stage is empirical, focusing on the physical elements in nature which can be studied scientifically. The physicality in this approach is like the body in the theory of archetypes. By studying the physical nature of life, we can better understand how it works and how it is evolving.

Despite the clear parallels between Comte's theory of intellectual progress and the theory of archetypes, it does not appear that there are other similarities. Comte's theory implies that the theological stage is less advanced than the metaphysical, and metaphysical less advanced than the positive. But, the theory of archetypes says the opposite- that spirit should prevail over the mind, and the mind over the body.

So, it appears that Comte's most famous theory does not have a strong parallel in the theory of archetypes. Its strongest parallels are in the theories of cerebral functioning and social progress. While this is somewhat disappointing, it does not negate the importance of the theory of archetypes to the overall pattern of Comte's theories.

THE THEORIES OF DURKHEIM

Durkheim is known for his theories in sociology, but also for the application of theory in his famous study of suicide. Durkheim believed that the causes of suicide were "primarily social rather than psychological or economic."[22] How a person relates to society and to others will affect the propensity toward suicide. Each social group "has a collective inclination for the act" and it is "made up of currents of egoism, altruism or anomy running through…society".[23] Thus, suicide may be one of three forms-egoistic, altruistic, or anomic.

Types of Suicide

Egoistic suicide results when "an individual experiences weakening of his commitments to group goals and norms, when he is thrown more upon his own resources."[24] Or, it may be viewed as "excessive individualism" which is "caused by the deficient authority of a *conscience collective* that is disintegrating."[25] Durkheim defined the conscience collective as the group mind, or how society as a whole thinks about social phenomena. In egoistic suicide, the collective power of society "is not sufficiently attractive and constructive to appeal to the vital and strong individual so that he is deprived of goals and directions."[26] In other words, "society is not present enough in the necessary amounts in the individual egos."[27] An existentialist view of the world might lead one to an egoistic suicide.

In terms of the theory of archetypes, egoistic suicide is related to the mind. In egoistic suicide, the mind turns in on itself and abandons meaningful social interaction. The individual finds little or no meaning in the collective aspirations of society or of his particular group, and decides that life is meaningless. Suicide is a form of self-expression, where the individual mind asserts its independence and expresses contempt for society and its values. So, egoistic suicide is an assertion of the mind over the body and spirit, choosing to end the life of the body and to defy the moral tenets of the spirit.

Altruistic suicide is "the opposite of egoistic. The ego is no longer the individual's own property, and he is deeply committed to the group's norms and goals."[28] Altruistic suicide arises from a "very high integration of the individual into the group, so that a person would sacrifice himself to avoid disturbances of it".[29] This type of suicide is found most often in primitive societies, where the importance of the group over the individual is stressed.

Durkheim notes that this type of suicide may occur from a "question of honor" or "purely for the joy of sacrifice, because, even with no particular reason, renunciation in itself is considered praiseworthy."[30] An example of this might be suicide among religious groups, as when Buddhist monks use self-immolation as a form of protest. Or, to use a more contemporary example, suicide bombers may seek praise and reward from Allah by killing the enemies of Islam.

It appears that altruistic suicide is motivated by a sense of duty or a higher calling. Thus, in terms of the theory of archetypes, it is linked with the spirit. The spirit of the group or the spirit of God calls one to commit suicide for the sake of glorifying oneself in the eyes of God or the group. It is believed that it also brings glory to God- altruism calls one to sacrifice oneself for what is perceived to be a greater good.

Anomic suicide arises when "rapid and extreme social change or crisis threatens the group norms of a society. An individual becomes uncertain of the appropriate behavior demanded of him and experiences a state of anomie."[31] In other words, it occurs when "individuals are caught between conflicting or inconsistent norms".[32] Both egoistic and anomic suicide "spring from the fact that society is not present in the necessary amounts in the individual egos."[33]

In the case of anomic suicide, society gives no "creative strength" to the individual, nor does he receive "moral direction and meaning"[34] from society. Durkheim saw a "definite correlation between anomic suicide and the free capitalistic society with its grim and unregulated competition, its crises and depressions".[35] This kind of tragedy reflects a moral vacuum in contemporary societies.

Recent studies have shown that anomic suicide increases "in times both of sharp economic depression and of exceptional prosperity."[36] During times of prosperity, normlessness becomes more common, because wealth is acquired without hard work and poverty is experienced despite proper values and hard work . Recent studies also show that anomic suicide varies within groups in society. Married men are less prone to this type of suicide than bachelors, according to one study. Bachelors are more "easily disenchanted with life"[37] than married men, and hence more prone to anomic suicide.

Anomic suicide is like the body in the theory of archetypes. The body follows the directions of the mind and spirit in performing its physical tasks. But without the direction of the mind or spirit, the body lacks incentive to continue its activities; it performs its duties without joy or purpose. Such a state of existence leads to anomie, depression, and the desire to put an end to life.

Other Theories

Durkheim is best known for his research on suicide, but his other theories in sociology are an important influence in the field. In particular, his concepts of social facts, collective consciousness, and institutions are influential, and related to each other in a way that conforms to the theory of archetypes.

For Durkheim, the "proper study of sociology was the study of social facts, which exist and which can and ought to be conceived as independent of psychological facts, or the person."[38] Social facts are the collective representations of society which characterize the nature of social interaction, rather than individuals. Social facts, or collective representations, are "originated by society, but apparently have a life of their own and are capable of acting and developing according to laws of evolution of their own."[39]

Social facts are the basic units of analysis in sociology. In terms of methodology, Durkheim wrote that we should "treat social facts as things"[40] to be observed and analyzed. In advanced societies, social facts include complex phenomena such as legal codes, social statistics, and religious dogma.[41] In primitive societies, social facts are found in simpler form, in religious ceremonies, tribal customs and various modes of individual interaction.

Social facts are like the body in the theory of archetypes. They are the driving force in society, a group of habitual ways of doing things which society agrees upon. Like the body, they can be observed and analyzed to draw conclusions about the workings of the mind. The mind in this case is the collective mind of society, which creates these collective representations or social facts. Social facts, like the body, obey the group mind and produce actions which are consistent with the values of society.

If social facts are like the body, then the collective consciousness is like the mind. According to Durkheim, a society "manifests a collective consciousness, or group mind, which gives rise to collective representations and the institutions which depend on the latter."[42] The laws of the group mind can be "studied independently through an analysis of its collective representations."[43] In other words, collective representations are the product of the collective consciousness, and the collective consciousness of a society may be analyzed by understanding its collective representations or social facts.

Durkheim was interested in studying the contemporary group mind through an analysis of social facts, but he also believed that the study of anthropology sheds light on the contemporary mind, by analyzing more primitive modes of thought. He believed that "contemporary 'reason' is 'collective,' and that if we are to comprehend its nature, we must understand the 'primitive' strata that have gone into its making."[44] For Durkheim, the study of primitive modes of thought "was always directed toward shedding light upon the contemporary mind; he emphasized the aspect of continuity."[45]

The relationship between the mind and body is similar to the relationship between the group mind and social facts. Just as the mind directs to body to act and produce physical results, so the group mind directs the production of social facts. While social facts are collective ideas and not actual physical reality, they are the substance of sociology and the essence of social interaction. While the mind directs the body, it also responds to feedback from the body in making its decisions. Similarly, the group mind responds to social facts which affect society, either positively or negatively. If society is prospering, the group mind continues to operate in the status quo; if society is declining, the group mind seeks reasons for that decline and makes adjustments to reverse the negative trend.

In the writings of Durkheim, the relationship between the group mind and social facts is not perfectly clear. David Bidney writes: "What the relationship is between the collective mind and its collective representations, we are not told."[46] Perhaps this relationship could be clarified by an application of the theory of archetypes. The relationship between mind and body serves as an archetype for the relationship between the collective mind and its collective representations.

The final element in the equation is institutions. Institutions are a product of the collective consciousness or group mind. Institutions were so important to Durkheim that he used them in his definition of sociology, which he defined as "the science of institutions."[47] Other sociologists write that through its institutions, a society "reveals itself to the observer in all its complexity and variability."[48] From the viewpoint of anthropology and history, institutions are "the organs that conserve what is best in the past of the human race."[49]

Durkheim observed that institutions were similar in different societies, because they performed similar social functions. But historically, as societies developed, certain institutions became more important than others.[50] For example, religious institutions were more important at one stage of development and social service institutions at another. For Durkheim, institutions were vital forms of organization that reflected the heart and soul of society.

In the theory of archetypes, the linkage between the spirit and institutions is self-evident. The spirit provides moral and ethical direction to the mind in its deliberations. Similarly, institutions provide moral and ethical direction to the group mind, providing needed correction if the group mind strays from important principles and ideals. Institutions are noted for their stability, and that stability provides a moral compass for the changing ideas of the group mind.

At the same time, institutions should not be heavy-handed in guiding the activities of the group mind. Society should be allowed to evolve, to adapt to changing social conditions without undue influence from oppressive institutions. Institutions must change as society changes, but their underlying mission of providing for basic human needs should not change. The analogy between institutions and the spirit of man is rich with comparison.

CONCLUSIONS

This chapter has applied the theory of archetypes to the sociological theories of Comte and Durkheim. Table 5 summarizes that application. Comte's theories are numerous and complex, but many of them have a common thread in their tripartite nature. One of his foundational theories- the theory of cerebral functioning- is a direct parallel to the theory of archetypes, and argues that man's perception of mind, body and spirit directly influence social progress and human history.

Table 5. Sociology and the Theory of Archetypes

Comte
Mind/Intellectual progress
Intellectual progress is like the mind, because it represents a social development in which ideas are highly valued. Intellectual progress elevates the mind and its products above all other values.
Body/Material progress
Material progress is like the body, because it is progress of a physical nature. Material progress places greatest importance on increasing the wealth and material prosperity of a society.

Table 5 (con't)

Spirit/Moral progress Moral progress is like the spirit, because it emphasizes the development of morality and ethics in a society. When moral progress is highly valued, the behavior and ethics of citizens are elevated above material and intellectual progress.
Durkheim
Mind/Egoistic suicide Egoistic suicide is like the mind, because it occurs when the mind isolates itself and fails to find meaning in societal values and norms. Suicide is a form of self-expression, where the individual mind asserts independence from society and its values.
Body/Anomic Suicide Anomic suicide is like the body, because individuals are caught between inconsistent and conflicting norms. The normal controls by the mind and spirit are gone, and the body finds itself without moral direction and meaning.
Spirit/Altruistic suicide Altruistic suicide is like the spirit, because the ethics and morality of a particular group are placed above social norms. Individuals feel compelled to defend the values of their particular group by sacrificing their lives for "spiritual" values.
Mind/Group mind The group mind is like the mind, because it is the collective consciousness of society. It directs the thinking and action of a society, and determines which social facts and habits of interaction are most important.
Body/Social facts Social facts are like the body, because they are the physical evidence of accepted forms of human interaction. They are a group of habitual ways of doing things which society agrees upon. Social facts obey the group mind, and produce actions consistent with the values of society.
Spirit/Institutions Institutions are like the spirit, because they provide moral and ethical direction to the group mind. Institutions provide stability and needed correction if the group mind strays from important principles and ideals.

The theory of archetypes might add to our understanding of Comte's theory of social progress. *Material progress* is like the body, progress of a physical nature. Material progress is good, as it advances society through industrialization and technology, but material progress can have a darker side, if human beings become materalistic, vulgar and crass. The possession of goods can make people indifferent to higher values in life, i.e. to spiritual fulfillment, intellectual achievement, and cultural advancement. Just as dominance by the body can hurt the spirit and the mind, so dominance by material progress can hinder the true advancement of a society.

Intellectual progress has a parallel in its emphasis on the mind in the theory of archetypes. If the mind if overly emphasized, the spirit can suffer and human life can lack the necessary moral direction. If intellectual progress becomes the clarion call, society may become indifferent to moral concerns. Morality may be redefined as relative, and its application a matter of intellectual judgment, depending upon circumstances and the preferences of individuals with their own independent judgments.

Moral progress also has a negative side. When the spirit is emphasized, to the detriment of mind and body, the result may be anti-intellectualism or aestheticism. When moral progress is the major goal, society becomes bound in ethical rules which inhibit the free expression of the human mind and spirit. The joy in life is diminished in a society that places the mind and body in an inferior, rather than complementary, position. That society also will decline in material progress, as aestheticism becomes a higher virtue.

Durkheim's theories also may be interpreted and enhanced through the theory of archetypes. Durkheim's theory of suicide posits three types- egoistic, altruistic and anomic. In this chapter, I have argued that egoistic suicide is related to the mind, altruistic to the spirit, and anomic to the body. If that is true, then the causes of those types of suicide might be diagnosed and treated by society with greater efficacy. For example, if egoistic suicide is a major problem in society, then emphasis on the mind is too strong in that society. It may indicate that there is a serious lack of spiritual values to restrain the individual from committing suicide. That society may need more spiritual, ethical and moral teaching to prevent suicide.

When altruistic suicide becomes the major pattern in a society, then spiritual and moral values are too dominant. Individuals focus too much on the rewards of the afterlife, and not enough on the preservation of the mind and body to do good deeds on earth. In a sense, spiritual values are distorted in altruistic suicide, and there is a lack of common sense and reason in society. Wrong values need to be corrected, along with renewed emphasis on the importance of material and intellectual progress.

If society suffers from a prevalence of anomic suicide, the body is overly emphasized. Society is lacking in both moral and intellectual controls, so individuals feel lacking in purpose and without direction. That society needs a more inspiring educational system and a stronger way of imparting moral values to its citizens. When the proper values are restored to individuals, society will have direction and purpose, and anomic suicide should decline.

The other theory of Durkheim discussed in this chapter relates to his concepts of social facts, the group mind and institutions. Social facts were related to the body, the group mind related to mind, and institutions to the spirit. Social facts are the basic social elements in society, the collective results of the interactions of people in a society. They are like the body in that they are the physical, empirical data that tell us about a society. As the body should obey the mind, so should social facts be an accurate reflection of the group mind, what Durkheim calls the collective consciousness. Whenever there are dysfunctions in society, sociologists should examine this linkage carefully, to determine if and why social facts are not following the direction of the group mind.

The group mind, like the mind in the individual, should guide and direct society in the production of social facts (the actions of the body). But, as the mind is responsive to input from the body, so the group mind should be responsive to social facts and their natural force. Social facts, like the body, are a powerful force in society and occasionally must be able to lead the group mind in a particular direction. If the group mind is sufficiently aware of the nature of social facts, it can greatly enhance cooperation between the two.

Finally, institutions are like the spirit in that they provide moral and ethical guidance for the group mind. Just as the spirit must avoid too much interference in the operations of the mind, so institutions must avoid dominating the group mind in its workings and production of social facts. Institutions should confine their role in society to providing corrective action when the group mind is going off course. They are the principal source of moral values in society, a force that corrects the natural tendencies in men to seek after their own interests.

NOTES

[1] Ritchie P. Lowry. *Sociology: The Science of Society*. (New York: Scribner, 1969), 9.
[2] Ibid., 11.
[3] Murray F. Leaf. *Man, Mind, and Science: A History of Anthropology*. (New York: Columbia University Press), 2.
[4] Gorge Ritzer. *Sociological Theory*. (New York: Alfred A. Knopf, 1983), 223.
[5] Ibid., 12-13.
[6] Harry E. Barnes. "The Social and Political Philosophy of Auguste Comte: Positivist Utopia and the Religion of Humanity." *An Introduction to the History of Sociology*. Harry E. Barnes (Ed.). (Chicago: University of Chicago Press, 1948), 86.
[7] Ibid., 108.
[8] Ibid., 93.
[9] Ibid., 92.
[10] Ibid., 93.
[11] Auguste Comte. *A General View of Positivism*. (New York: Robert Speller & Sons, 1957), 7.
[12] Ibid., 8.
[14] Barnes, op. cit., 99.
[15] Comte, op. cit., 9.
[16] Ibid., 9.
[17] Barnes.op. cit., 93.
[18] Ibid., 93.
[19] Comte, op. cit., 3.
[20] Kenneth Thompson. Auguste Comte: *The Foundation of Sociology*. (New York: John Wiley & Sons, 1975), 40.
[21] Ibid., 13.
[22] Samuel Koenig. Sociology: *An Introduction to the Science of Society*. (New York: Barnes & Noble, 1972), 62.
[23] Ritzer, op. cit., 103.
[24] Lowry, op. cit., 13.
[25] Albert Salomon. "The Legacy of Durkheim." *Emile Durkheim 1858-1917*. Kurt H. Wolff (Ed.). (New York: Arno Press, 1979), 259.
[26] Ibid., 260.
[27] Ibid., 260.
[28] Lowry, op. cit., 13.
[29] Leaf, op. cit., 157.
[30] Emile Durkheim. *Suicide: A Study in Sociology*. George Simpson (Ed.). (New York: Free Press, 1951), 223.
[31] Lowry, op. cit., 14.
[32] Leaf, op. cit., 157.
[33] Salomon, op. cit., 260.
[34] Ibid., 260.
[35] Ibid., 260.
[36] Emile Benoit-Smullyan. "The Sociologism of Emile Durkheim and His School." *An Introduction to the History of Sociology*. Harry E. Barnes (Ed.). (Chicago: University of Chicago Press, 1948), 509.
[37] Ibid., 509-510.
[38] Neil J. Smelser. *Sociology*. (Cambridge, MA: Blackwell, 1994), 12.
[39] David Bidney. *Theoretical Anthropology*. (New York: Columbia University Press, 1953), 92.
[40] Benoit-Smullyan, op. cit., 501.
[41] Ibid., 502.
[42] Bidney, op. cit., 92.

[43] Ibid., 92.
[44] Joseph Neyer. "Individualism and Socialism in Durkheim." *Emile Durkheim 1858-1917*. Kurt H. Wolff (Ed.). (New York: Arno Press, 1979), 34.
[45] Ibid., 34.
[46] Bidney, op. cit., 92.
[47] Koenig, op. cit., 2.
[48] Ibid., 69.
[49] Ibid., 69.
[50] Paul Bohannan. "Conscience Collective and Culture." *Emile Durkheim 1858-1917*. Kurt H. Wolff (Ed.). (New York: Arno Press, 1979), 54.

Chapter 6

ANTHROPOLOGY

Anthropology and sociology are closely related fields, and the theoretical approaches are similar. Durkheim is quoted by sociologists and by anthropologists for his theories and his study of suicide. One of the authors mentioned in this chapter, William Graham Sumner, is a noted sociologist, but his work also has important implications for anthropology. So, the two fields share a number of commonalities.

Yet, anthropology as a discipline is different from sociology. According to one anthropologist, it is "a broad and complex discipline that studies man in all of his biological, social and cultural dimensions."[1] It has two major divisions- physical and cultural (or social) anthropology- but archeology is often included in academic departments of anthropology. Thus, one might say there are three major divisions in the field. From a theoretical perspective, modern anthropology is "functional, historical, diffusionist, psychological, and comparative; in other words it has developed into an eclectic discipline."[2] There are numerous theoretical approaches in the field.

This chapter will concentrate on two theorists who have had a seminal influence. First, the important work of Franz Boaz will be explored and applied to the theory of archetypes. Boaz is widely considered to be "the father of American anthropology," and his concepts of historical, psychological and environmental conditions are seminal in the field. Then, the major theories of Sumner will be examined in light of the theory of archetypes. Sumner's concepts of folkways, mores and institutions are important to the study of different cultures in modern society.

THE THEORIES OF *BOAZ*

Franz Boaz was a reluctant theorist. In fact, he often was criticized for "failure to generalize from his findings."[3] In his own defense, Boaz replied that while the ultimate goal of anthropology was to formulate general laws about culture, "first it would be necessary to have more detailed studies of tribal cultures and histories."[4] He preferred to develop theories inductively, only after a careful examination of the facts.

Boaz developed and applied the concept of cultural relativism to anthropology. During his time, cultural evolutionists were arguing that culture evolved over time from simple societies to complex industrial societies. Simple societies were regarded as inferior to modern Western culture. Boaz argued that societies were "unique entities that could not be compared."[5] The value of a culture should not be diminished by comparing it with another culture that is more economically advanced.

But, perhaps the greatest contribution of Boaz was the idea that cultural customs could be explained from the perspectives of psychological factors, environmental conditions and historical connections. Of these three, he believed that historical connections were most important. In fact, Boaz believed that "culture must be primarily understood in a historical context."[6]

The most basic factors affecting a culture are environmental conditions. Boaz believed that the environment could affect not only the culture, but also the physical characteristics of cultures, in terms of race. He demonstrated that the characteristics of the Caucasian, Negroid and Mongoloid races "are not constant but change with environmental conditions".[7] Boaz found, for example, that "the head form of children of European immigrants in America deviates markedly from that of their parents."[8]

Environmental conditions also affect cultural customs. During the time of Boaz, anthropology emphasized the importance of environmental conditions in the shaping of divergent cultures. In his famous book, *Race, Language and Culture*, Boaz writes that environmental conditions have "a certain limited effect upon the culture of man," but they are not "the primary molder of culture".[9] Boaz wrote that "A hasty review of the tribes and peoples of our globe shows that people most diverse in culture and language live under the same geographical conditions".[10] Thus, environmental factors are not a strong determining force in the development of cultural customs.

A stronger influence on cultural customs is psychological factors. Psychological factors influence the ideas that shape a culture. Boaz believed that "a clear enunciation of the elementary idea gives us the psychological reason for its existence."[11] For example, in certain cultures, the concept of the afterlife is referred to as "the land of shadows." The fact that "the land of shadows is so often placed in the west suggests the endeavor to localize it at the place where the sun and stars vanish."[12] There is a psychological reason for the idea.

Psychological factors affect cultural customs principally through ideas, but psychology as a discipline also affects anthropology and the study of culture. Boaz wrote that "particular attention is now being paid to the mental status of primitive man and of mental life under pathological conditions."[13] Psychological factors in primitive man affected the development of culture, and cultures could be studied from this psychological perspective.

Historical connections are the strongest influence on cultural customs, according to Boaz's theory. All customs and traditions in a culture have historical depth- some are older than others- but they have a common ground in the history of that culture. In fact, without historical traditions and customs, culture would not exist. Hence, historical connections are the primary basis for cultural customs. History provides "an internal comparative analysis, which brings out the components of a culture without the difficulties of arbitrary comparisons between unrelated groups."[14]

Historical connections can reveal other factors affecting customs, such as environmental and psychological factors. Boaz believed that "historical explanations stood as complementary to psychology, culture contact, or environmental adaptation."[15] By a proper understanding of the history of a culture, its environmental and psychological aspects can be more completely understood.

Boaz's theory is related to the theory of archetypes, but the connections may not be as strong as in other theories from other disciplines. Clearly, psychological factors are related to the mind. In the theory of archetypes, the mind directs the body, makes decisions, and listens to the spirit in matters of ethical import. In Boaz's theory, psychological factors affect cultural customs on a regular basis through ideas, which direct the formation of traditions and customs in a society. Psychological factors help to decide which customs are most important, and how culture should change on a daily basis.

Environmental conditions are like the body in the theory of archetypes. The body is the driving physical force that accomplishes tasks for the mind and spirit. It is subservient to both, yet its input is important to the decisions of both. Environmental conditions affect cultural customs in a physical way. They do not determine the customs, as psychological factors and historical connections do, but they are the physical mechanism that is used to create change. The physical environment of a culture allows certain ideas to flourish and others to wither away. For example, in a warm climate an afternoon nap may become a cultural custom, but when the climate changes with the advent of air conditioning, the idea behind the custom may become obsolete. History can be reversed by a simple technological change.

Just as the body provides input to the mind and spirit, so environmental conditions provide input to psychological factors and historical connections. The environment may force the thinking of society to change and the traditional ways of doing things to be set aside. The environment, through its daily influence of enabling customs to continue, occasionally prompts a change in those customs in a powerful way.

Historical connections are like the spirit in the theory of archetypes. They determine the overall direction of a culture and are the "spirit" behind the culture. Just as the spirit provides ethical and moral guidance to the mind and body, historical connections provide the ultimate direction in a particular culture. They determine which customs are worthy of elevation to a higher status and which customs are of lesser importance.

Like the spirit in its relations with the mind, historical connections should not interfere with the operations of psychological factors, as those factors influence a culture. History and the continuation of traditional customs should not take precedence over original ideas that may benefit a society. Customs must be allowed to change as psychological factors and ideas change in a society. The theory of archetypes helps to draw limits on the power of historical connections in their future influence on a culture.

THE THEORIES OF *SUMNER*

William G. Sumner's major theoretical contribution to anthropology and sociology is his concepts of folkways, mores and institutions. According to one sociologist, Sumner "contributed one of the most fruitful and clarifying analyses of culture and its implications."[16] Another observes that his theory is "one of the finest treatments of a special field of sociology."[17] Sumner's theory of folkways contributes to both sociology and anthropology, because it sheds light on both contemporary society and comparative cultures.

Folkways are "customary ways of behaving and acting which arise automatically within a group to meet the problems of living."[18] They are the "ways of the folk" or customs which "grow unconsciously; they are not creations of purpose; but they are basic societal forces."[19] Sumner wrote that the "greatest and best example is language."[20] Language is a folkway that is constantly changing, a force in society and a method of solving problems. It operates unconsciously, and shapes the way that a society communicates.

Folkways can take other forms besides language. Typical folkways in a culture are group habits like shaking hands in greeting, driving on the right side of the road, and eating three meals a day. Folkways are so automatic and ingrained in our behavior that they are difficult to recognize as perhaps unique to contemporary civilization.

In terms of the theory of archetypes, folkways are like the body. They are the physical ways in which a culture or society expresses itself. Folkways, like the body, are driven by habits and perform activities automatically. They are actions that solve problems in a culture, in communication, and in various forms of social interaction. Like the body, folkways are a driving force that accomplishes the goals of a particular culture; they are the social interactions that occur on a daily basis.

If folkways are like the body in the theory of archetypes, mores are like the mind. Mores are "folkways which are thought by the group to be indispensable to its welfare and the violation of which is believed to endanger existence."[21] Mores are a type of folkway that has evolved over time, because of its importance. When folkways "reach the stage at which they are raised to the level of conscious reflection and are regarded as adapted to securing the continued welfare and prosperity of the group, they thereby become transformed into mores."[22]

Like the mind, mores are a conscious reflection on how to protect a culture and make it prosper. Mores consist of decisions made by a culture to perform certain acts to protect and sustain itself. Like the mind directing the body, mores direct the operation of folkways in a culture, elevating some to greater importance than others. Mores "determine what shall be regarded as right or wrong modes of conduct in any group,"[23] and the violation of mores may result in "severe punishment."[24]

Mores "are not laws, though they may produce laws."[25] Examples of mores include monogamy, democracy, collective bargaining, and "nearly all of our beliefs and practices concerned with moral values."[26] Mores are like the mind in the theory of archetypes, because they impose order on society, and require that group practices in a culture be for the benefit of the whole culture.

Mores have a moral component that gives them certain qualities of the spirit, as expressed in the theory of archetypes. But, they are not associated with the spirit because, like the mind regulating the actions of the body, mores actively and daily regulate the folkways in a society. Unlike the spirit, they do not occasionally intervene to influence the mind or body, but are active participants in the ongoing process of cultural interaction. It is true that moral values come form mores, but they also come from the third element in Sumner's theory- from institutions.

According to Sumner, a "vital activity or interest surrounded by a cluster of folkways and mores is an *institution*."[27] Sumner, in his book *Folkways*, describes an institution "as consisting not only of a concept, idea, or interest, but of a structure as well."[28] This structure implies an "apparatus or a group of functionaries" through which an idea "takes on concrete form and is put to work to serve the needs of society."[29]

Institutions can take various forms. There are economic and governmental institutions, religious institutions, recreational institutions, institutions for esthetic and intellectual expressions, and family institutions, such as courtship, marriage and divorce.[29] Sumner wrote that institutions can be divided into two types: "*crescive*, or those developing gradually through the process of accretion, and *enacted*, or those appearing as a result of conscious and rational effort."[30] An example of the former is the state, and of the latter is a college or bank.

Sumner himself was trained as a political scientist, so much of his discussion of institutions is related to political institutions. Political institutions replaced religious institutions as ultimate sources of authority in society following the Renaissance and the Enlightenment. Sumner wrote that in the nineteenth century many of the "abstract notions about rights" which were formulated in religious institutions were "reduced to actuality in constitutions, laws, and judicial rulings."[31] He praised political institutions as sources of morality, but he was not sanguine about the possibilities of corruption in those institutions. He wrote that there are numerous examples "to prove that constitutional institutions of the best type fall into corruption and decay unless the virtues of political self-control exist in high vigor and purity in the mores of the society."[32] Thus, good institutions are dependent upon good mores in society.

In terms of the theory of archetypes, institutions are like the human spirit. Like the spirit, institutions are not a directive force in society but more a corrective one. When a culture begins to stray from its underlying ethical and moral principles, institutions exert a correcting influence. For example, democracy is a moral force that guides American government, but occasionally it comes into conflict with economic mores relating to free enterprise. Specifically, private economic interests may seek laws that are opposed by the majority. Congress or the courts may be forced to limit economic freedoms for the sake of preserving the rights of the majority. Institutions in the federal government occasionally must intervene to protect the important moral values of the culture.

Institutions also are like the spirit in that they must work in cooperation with folkways and mores. As the spirit listens to the mind and body, so institutions must operate within existing folkways and mores. If institutions are created which work against current mores, the culture will suffer. This was the case when prohibition laws were enacted in the United States. Prohibition created moral restraints that were not compatible with American culture. Most Americans believed that drinking, in moderation, was not a vice. The culture also prized mores relating to freedom of the individual to make moral choices without undue interference from the state.

In the case of prohibition, illegal sources of alcoholic beverages were developed to accommodate the folkways and mores of American culture. Organized crime gained a strong foothold in American society, providing for the illegal desires of the American people. To some extent, American society is still recovering from that mistake- organized crime has declined, but it is still in existence. So, institutions must be careful about how they intervene in society, especially when that intervention goes against existing folkways and mores.

CONCLUSIONS

In this chapter, the theories of Boaz and Sumner have been examined. The application of the theory of archetypes is presented in Table 6. Boaz was not known for his theoretical work, but his theory of the three influences on cultural customs is seminal in anthropology. Cultural customs in a society are influenced by psychological factors, environmental conditions and historical connections. As this chapter points out, the three influences are related to the theory of archetypes.

Table 6. Anthropology and the Theory of Archetypes

Boaz *Mind/Psychological factors* Psychological factors are like the mind, because they affect cultural customs on a regular basis and direct the formation of traditions and customs in a society. They also help to determine which customs are most important. *Body/Environmental conditions* Environmental conditions are like the body, because they affect cultural customs in a physical way. They are the physical mechanism that is used to create change, the physical environment that allows certain ideas to flourish and others to die.

Table 6 (con't)

Spirit/Historical connections
Historical connections are like the spirit, because they determine the overall direction of a culture. As the spirit of a culture, which is embodied in its past, they determine the relative importance of past and future customs.
Sumner
Mind/Mores
Mores are like the mind, because they consist of conscious decisions made by a culture to protect and sustain itself. Mores direct the operation of folkways in a culture, elevating some to greater importance than others.
Body/Folkways
Folkways are like the body, because they are the physical ways in which a culture expresses itself. They are actions that solve problems in a culture, and social interactions that occur on a daily basis.
Spirit/Institutions
Institutions are like the spirit, because they provide moral and ethical direction to a culture. They should correct a culture from moving in the wrong direction, but should not interfere with the daily operations of folkways and mores.

Psychological factors are like the mind, because they are based on the use of ideas to influence cultural customs. Just as the mind uses ideas to influence the body and spirit, so psychological factors use ideas in the process of guiding a culture. Like the mind, psychological factors help to decide, direct and actively control cultural change. They form the content of decisions about culture, then they either allow customs to continue or change the customs to suit the new psychological reality. The mind of man and psychology influence customs in the culture on a moment-by-moment basis.

Environmental conditions are like the body in the theory of archetypes. Like the body, they are the physical mechanism used to create change in a culture. Environmental conditions work automatically, like habits in the body, to permit the expression of cultural customs. Some environments are more conducive to certain ideas than to others, so its response to psychological factors helps to shape the emergence of new customs, or allow the continuance of old customs. Environmental conditions provide input to psychological factors and ideas, much as the body provides input to the mind.

Historical connections are like the spirit in terms of archetypes. One might say that historical connections are the spirit of society, because they provide the heart and soul of a culture. They give overall direction to cultures by moral and ethical guidance, and relating customs of the past with customs of the future. They not like the mind, which is a directive force in society, but are more a corrective force. They correct ideas that are not in keeping with the best traditions of a society, the best cultural customs of the past. For that reason, Boaz believed they were the most important influences in the creation of cultural customs.

The theories of Sumner were influential in both anthropology and sociology. His theory of folkways is expressed in the concepts of folkways, mores and institutions. These three factors are the basic forces in a society or culture that determine its focus and direction.

Folkways are like the body in that they are basic social forces that form the substance of social interaction. Like habits in the body, folkways are unconscious forms of social practice, like language or the habit of shaking hands in greeting. They are performed daily, and even moment-by-moment in various forms of social interaction. Like the body, they provide input back to the force that directs them, in order to make alterations in the different forms of social practice.

The directive force, in this case, is mores. Mores are like the mind in that they guide the folkways and give preeminence to certain forms of social interaction. Mores are a conscious reflection on what are the most important folkways, and how they can be used to protect society. Mores impose order in society and act daily to influence the direction of social interaction. Examples of mores include principles like democracy and monogamy.

And finally, institutions are like the spirit in the theory of archetypes. Institutions are structures in a culture that emphasize certain ideals or moral principles. They are not a directive force, like mores, but a corrective one that keeps mores on track. Institutions provide the occasional intervention that is necessary for moral and ethical influences in society to prevail. Institutions work best when they cooperate with folkways and mores, and allow normal human interaction to take place without interference. Just as the spirit corrects the mind and body in their operations, so institutions are the corrective force in a culture.

NOTES

[1] Lowell D. Holmes. *Anthropology: An Introduction.* (New York: Ronald Press, 1971), 3.
[2] Ibid., 46.
[3] Ibid., 41.
[4] Ibid., 41.
[5] R. Jon McGee and Richard Warms. *Anthropological Theory: An Introductory History.* (Mountain View, CA: Mayfield Publishing Co., 1996), 129.
[6] Holmes, op. cit., 40.
[7] Samuel Koenig. *Sociology: An Introduction to the Science of Society.* (New York: Barnes & Noble, 1972), 31.

[8] Ibid., 31.
[9] Franz Boaz. *Race, Language and Culture*. (New York: The Free Press, 1940), 278.
[10] Ibid., 278.
[11] Murray F. Leaf. *A History of Anthropology: Man, Mind and Science*. (New York: Columbia University Press, 1979), 196.
[12] Ibid., 196.
[13] Boaz, op. cit., 244.
[14] Leaf, op. cit., 196.
[15] Ibid., 197.
[16] Koenig, op. cit., 44.
[17] Harry E. Barnes. "William Graham Sumner: Spencerianism in American Dress." *An Introduction to the History of Sociology*. Harry E. Barnes (Ed.). (Chicago: University of Chicago Press, 1949), 157.
[18] Koenig, op. cit., 44.
[19] A. L. Kroeber. *Anthropology*. (New York: Harcourt, Brace and Co., 1948), 266.
[20] William G. Sumner. *War and Other Essays*. Albert G. Keller (Ed.). (New York: Ams Press, 1970), 150.
[21] Koenig, op. cit., 45-46.
[22] Barnes, op. cit., 158.
[23] Ibid., 158.
[24] Koenig, op. cit., 46.
[25] Kroeber, op. cit., 266.
[26] Koenig, op. cit., 46.
[27] Ibid., 47.
[28] Ibid, 69.
[29] Ibid., 69.
[29] Ibid., 71.
[30] Ibid., 72.
[31] Sumner, op. cit., 158.
[32] Ibid., 163.

Chapter 7

CONCLUSIONS

The theory of archetypes is a new theory for the social sciences. In essence, in says that man's perception of his mind, body and spirit has influenced his thinking in the social sciences since their origin. Social institutions have arisen which are based on the tripartite nature of man himself.

The mind is an archetype for directive forces in society, which initiate action and make decisions. The mind guides the body to act, plans activities for the future, and protects the health and well-being of the body. It is responsive to input from the body and spirit, and it acts for the benefit of both. The mind is an archetype for directive and intellectual forces in politics, economics, psychology, sociology and anthropology.

The body is an archetype for physical forces in society, which use physical force to achieve particular ends. The body acts in response to the directives of the mind and carries out plans that originate in thought. Often, the body acts habitually and repeats actions without the direct control of the mind, but the original plan for action begins with the mind. The body is a model for powerful forces in society that act to achieve visible goals in the social system, such as going to war, changing the economy, or altering the nature of social interaction.

The spirit is an archetype for moral and ethical forces in society, a corrective force that brings society back in line. The spirit usually lets the mind direct the activities of the body, but occasionally it intervenes when the mind is off track and violates ethical principles. Often, the spirit speaks through the heart of man, through the emotions, which powerfully express pleasure or dismay at the decisions of the mind. In the social system, the spirit is represented by forces and institutions that impartially judge actions in society, and recommend moral correction.

In this book, the theory of archetypes is applied to the major social sciences-politics, economics, psychology, sociology and anthropology. There are several uses for this theory in the social sciences. First, it can be used to diagnose and treat social ills. In the political sphere, the body is an archetype for the executive branch of government. When the executive becomes too strong, it is like the body when it dominates the intellect. The body must be controlled by the mind in human behavior, and similarly the executive must be directed by the legislature for democracy to function properly. Thus, when the executive becomes too strong, new ways must be found to assert the power of the legislature in guiding the executive.

A second use of the theory is in explaining the relationships between theoretical concepts in the social sciences. For example, in economics the prices that guide sales and purchases are like the mind, because they direct economic decisions about allocation. Prices directly affect wages, which are like the body. Wages are the driving force in the economic system that allows the purchase of goods and services. When wages exert too strong an influence over prices, they begin to create dysfunctions in the system. Corrective action needs to be taken, usually in the form of governmental intervention. The complex relationships between concepts in economics can be illuminated when the theory of archetypes is applied.

A third use of the theory is in developing hypotheses, which can be tested scientifically. Hypotheses are detailed applications of a theory to make it more useful, in this case to society. As the theory of archetypes is applied, the details of the relationships between mind, body and spirit should help to illuminate the relationships between important concepts in the social sciences. If man's thinking about society is related to his perception of himself, it could greatly advance our knowledge of society and lead to the solving of important social problems.

This chapter reiterates some of the major points that were made concerning the application of the theory of archetypes to the social sciences. This review should help the reader to see connections between concepts in the different social sciences. Also, a few additional points are made by way of conclusion. Table 7 summarizes the basic relationships.

Table 7. Summary: The Theory of Archetypes and the Social Sciences

Discipline	Mind	Body	Spirit
Politics	Legislature	Executive	Judiciary
Economics	Prices & Demand	Wages & Supply	Taxes & Regulation
Psychology	Ego & Stimulus	Id & Response	Superego & Reinforcement
Sociology	Intellectual progress, Egoistic suicide & Group mind	Material progress, Anomic suicide & Social facts	Moral progress, Altruistic suicide & Institutions
Anthropology	Psychological Factors & Mores	Environmental conditions & Folkways	Historical connections & Institutions

POLITICS

The writings of Plato show a clear connection between the theory of archetypes and government. Plato writes in *The Republic* that the mind, body and spirit are related to the three functions of government. While his three functions of government are similar to the three branches of government in the United States, there are some differences. The important point is that Plato believed that man's perception of himself served as an archetype for the government that he created.

The mind is related to the legislature, because both are responsible for decisions that guide and direct either the body or the body politic. Madison and Hamilton wrote in *The Federalist* that the legislature should be the dominant branch of government, and that it should be responsible for the overall direction of the political system. The men who make up the legislature should be knowledgeable about public affairs and have a will to represent the people. In making their decisions, they should be acutely aware of the political environment and be willing to work with the executive branch. As the mind works with the body, so the legislature must be willing to work with the executive in a cooperative fashion.

The executive branch of government is like the body in that it is the physical force in society that accomplishes the tasks of government. Hamilton wrote that the executive should be energetic, and that his main task was the physical preservation of the republic. Like the body, the executive wields the physical power of the state and acts for its benefit and prosperity. But as the body is subordinate to the mind, so the executive should be subordinate to the legislature, the ultimate authority in political society. The best executive is energetic yet subordinate to the legislature.

The spirit is like the judicial branch of government in that both are devoted to the application of ethics and mortality in a fair and impartial manner. The judiciary hears cases and controversies between parties, and makes decisions based on law and precedent, which is a form of codified morality. Like the spirit, the judiciary should not be an intrusive force in society, but only assert itself when the legislative or executive branches are off track. The judiciary should the ultimate authority in political society, but it should be a corrective rather than a directive force in public policy.

When the three branches of government are working as they should in a cooperative way, society greatly benefits and political freedoms are preserved. However, when one branch becomes dominant or fails to perform its vital functions, society as a whole suffers. When the executive branch is too strong, tyranny and dictatorship are the result. When the legislative branch is too strong, government may suffer from weakness manifested in the inability to protect itself or to pursue an appropriate foreign policy. When the judicial branch is too strong, society may suffer from a form of moral tyranny where a small group of individuals dictates values to society which are contrary to social well-being.

The theory of archetypes can help to diagnose these problems, and prescribe remedies for them. The theory also can be used to deal with more subtle problems that interfere with the smooth operation of government. In public administration, for example, one of the perennial questions is: Should administration be separated from politics? Does politics interfere with the impartial application of laws and policies by administrators? Understanding the proper relationship between the mind and body may help to deal with that problem. Political factors commonly influence the legislative process, so the legislature is the usual source of political influence on administrators. In certain circumstances, that influence should be diminished, and in others it should be allowed to increase. It is a matter of balance, just as the mind's influence over the body must be balanced with the body's abilities to carry out its functions.

ECONOMICS

The theory of archetypes, as applied to micro-economics, says that the mind is like prices, the body is like wages, and the spirit like taxes. Prices guide the decisions of consumers and overall decisions of the economic system. They are directive forces that determine what new goods and services will be produced. Like the mind, prices consciously determine whether a business will thrive or fail, based on an analysis of their position of competitiveness relative to other businesses. Prices have an analytical component in that they represent thinking about what will succeed in the marketplace.

Wages are like the body, because they represent the physical force that allows the micro-economic system to work. Money is placed in the hands of workers and employees, who then spend money for goods and services based on personal needs and prices. Wages create spending and allow the economic system to operate. They drive production and influence prices as consumers exercise their preferences in consumption. Wages also result in savings and investment, which ordinarily have a beneficial effect on the economy. Savings and investment create new opportunities for production, giving new energy to the economy.

Taxes are like the spirit in the theory of archetypes, as they perform ethical and moral functions in the economy. Taxes redistribute wealth, allowing the alleviation of poverty and taking money from those who can afford it most. Taxes also pay for public goods which contribute to the well-being of all citizens, in the form of roads, police and fire protection, the regulation of commerce, etc. Taxes may not seem moral or ethical to those who have to pay, but their purpose in society is a moral one. They create more equality among citizens and promote freedom by giving all citizens the services which enhance their lives. In Jefferson's words, they allow the pursuit of happiness for all.

In macro-economics, the concepts of supply, demand and regulation also are related to the theory of archetypes. Demand is like the mind, as it guides and directs the system of production. Like the mind, demand helps to make decisions that control the overall operation of the economic system. Supply is like the body, which responds to demand and physically provides goods and services. Like the body, supply provides useful feedback to new demands in the economy, and allows them to alter their course if demand for the good or service is unrealistic.

Regulation in macro-economics is like the spirit in its essential quality of providing fairness to producers and consumers in the economy. An unregulated capitalist economy is capable of working many injustices, and regulation helps to maintain ethics and morality in the system. Government intervention ensures fairness, ethics, and overall survival of the economy.

The theory of archetypes may be particularly useful in the field of economics, because economic concepts are complex and highly interrelated. A simple analogy to the mind, body and spirit may help to sort out complex interrelations that defy diagnosis. In human beings, a proper balance between mind, body and spirit is vital to health and proper functioning. The theory of archetypes may help to maintain stability in the economic sphere, avoiding the dual problems of inflation and recession.

Psychology

The field of psychology in the twentieth century was greatly influenced by the theories of Freud and the behavioral theorists. In this book, the work of B.F. Skinner is used to represent the behavioral school, in particular his theory of operant conditioning. These theories are the foundation for modern psychology in the twenty-first century.

Freud's theory of personality is seminal to his work and highly related to the theory of archetypes. Freud posited that personality consists of id, ego and superego. The id is like the body, because it represents primitive drives and instinctual behavior in man. The id is a powerful force that drives man to seek pleasure. The ego is like the mind, because it controls the id and moderates its pursuit of pleasure. Like the mind, the ego is rational and uses its higher faculties to direct physical drives into socially acceptable outlets. But, unlike the mind, the ego does not contain emotion and passion. For Freud, passion was found in the id.

The superego is like the spirit, because it is the conscience of man. It restrains the activities of both the ego and id to conform to a higher code of morality and ethics. Freud believed that the superego consisted of values learned in childhood from parents and other authority figures. So, it differs from the spirit in that it is not associated with a belief in God.

In the behavioral school of psychology, stimulus, response and reinforcement are key concepts. Stimulus is like the mind, because it provides direction to the process of learning. A stimulus guides and directs an organism to respond in a particular way, much as the mind directs the body to respond and act. The response is like the body, as it is often the physical reaction to a directive stimulus. Like the body, the response is the most visible evidence that something has occurred, that learning has taken place.

Reinforcement in behaviorism is like the spirit, because it provides corrective action. Skinner believed that reinforcement was a key element in operant conditioning, guiding the overall process of learning. Reinforcement has an ethical or moral aspect in that in guides stimulus and response to achieve a desired outcome. Ideally, that outcome should represent higher values in society and be associated with ethical research.

Psychology as a discipline can benefit from the theory of archetypes. It explains the basic forces in man's personality, perhaps better than Freud's theory of personality. It certainly has greater implications than Freud's theory for the development of other theories in psychology. The theory of archetypes also illuminates the relationship between basic concepts in behaviorism. It may cause psychology to reassess the moral and ethical implications of reinforcement in human learning. And, it also may encourage the further understanding of stimulus and response, in light of the relationship between mind and body.

Sociology

The theories of Comte and Durkheim are vitally important in the field of sociology. Comte is widely considered to be the father of sociology and Durkheim a major theorist, as well as one of the first to apply Comte's theories. Both have theories which relate directly to the theory of archetypes.

Comte's theory of cerebral functioning is a direct parallel to the theory of archetypes. In that theory, the mind is described as "intellect,' the body as "action," and the spirit as "feeling." Although Comte did not directly refer to the spirit, in the theory of archetypes the emotions are noted as a vehicle for expression of the spirit- the "heart" in Christian theology.

Comte's theory of cerebral functioning is directly related to his theory of social progress, which also has a strong parallel in the theory of archetypes. Material progress is like the body, as it refers to the physical advancement of a society. Intellectual progress is like the mind, since progress in intellectual endeavors requires use of the mind and the advancement of ideas. Moral progress is like the spirit, because it represents the advancement of ethics and morality in society. The theory of archetypes advocates a proper balance of mind, body and spirit, and the implications for Comte's theory are that types of progress also should be in balance. Intellectual progress should not become more important than material progress, and material progress should not be ignored to advance moral progress. Spirit should govern mind, and mind should govern body, but each should be allowed to express itself in a proper balance.

Durkheim's theory of suicide is perhaps his best-known work. The parallels with the theory of archetypes help in addressing the problems of suicide in society. Egoistic suicide is like the mind, in that the mind tends to dominate an individual's perception of himself and others. The values of society are discounted as meaningless, and the individual loses connection with others. Altruistic suicide is like the spirit, as the morality and ethics of the group become more important than the individual. Individuals are encouraged to sacrifice themselves and their identities for the well-being of the group and its ideals.

Anomic suicide is like the body in the theory of archetypes, because there is lack of both individual and social control in life. The body exists without norms to guide it, and lacks incentive to live, in the absence of intellectual or moral guidance. Hopelessness leads to suicide. Durkheim believed that all three types of suicide were socially determined, rather than being the product of individual psychological factors. Thus, the solution to suicide lies in reforming society and its influence on the individual. From the perspective of the theory of archetypes, suicide increases when there is a lack of balance in society, a proper ordering of the authority of mind, body and spirit.

In Durkheim's other theories, his concepts of social facts, group habits and institutions are important. Social facts are like the body in that they are the driving force in society, the habitual customs of a group. The group mind, or collective consciousness, is like the mind, because it guides and directs the activities of society, using ideas to change the nature of social facts. Institutions are like the spirit in providing moral direction to society, being a corrective force when society is going off track. Although institutions are potentially the most powerful force, they must not use their power to inhibit the free actions of the group mind in producing social facts. Once again, balance is necessary.

ANTHROPOLOGY

The theories of Boaz and Sumner are used in the chapter on anthropology to illustrate the theory of archetypes. Boaz is considered to be the father of American anthropology, and Sumner is noted in both anthropology and sociology for his theories related to folkways. In anthropology, the primary emphasis is on culture, rather than society, especially comparative cultures.

Boaz is known for several theories, but perhaps best-known for his theory on cultural customs. The three primary influences on cultural customs are psychological factors, environmental conditions and historical connections. Psychological factors are like the mind, because they are ideas that influence customs. They decide, direct and control the development of customs in a culture. Environmental conditions are like the body, as they are the physical mechanisms used to create change in a culture. They work automatically and unconsciously like habits, providing input to psychological factors as they influence customs.

Historical connections are like the spirit in that they guide society and give moral direction. Historical connections relate the past to the future, and allow the orderly change of customs, in accordance with the values of the past. They are a corrective force, which affects psychological factors in shaping contemporary culture. The theory of archetypes aids in the process of relating these factors. While historical connections, like the spirit, are the most powerful force, they must allow psychological factors to influence customs on a daily basis, as the mind controls the body. And environmental conditions, like the body, must be allowed to affect customs in their own way, yet be responsive to psychological factors, as the body is responsive to the mind.

Finally, in Sumner's work the concepts of folkways, mores and institutions are related to the theory of archetypes. Folkways are like the body in that they are the most visible forms of social practice. An example of a folkway is language, which is a physical expression of the important ideas of a culture. Mores are like the mind, because they are a directive force. Mores are a conscious reflection on the most important folkways, and an elevation of those folkways to essential mores in society. Democracy is a more that guides the culture and protects the essential rights of citizens.

Institutions are like the spirit in the theory of archetypes, because they are a corrective force. Sumner's ideas about institutions are similar to Durkheim's in that they are the foundation of a culture, and a means to moral and ethical stability in a society. Institutions, like the spirit, work best when they blend with folkways and mores, and provide only occasional correction. While they are the ultimate power in a culture, that power should be exercised with care and restraint.

I hope that the reader has found this brief book interesting. The theory of archetypes certain is a new and original idea. I think it is worth the effort to apply it to the social sciences, because it may yield significant results. I have not tried to apply it to the sciences or mathematics, since I do not feel competent in those areas. Perhaps scholars in those fields might apply it in the future. I believe it is a theory that comes not only from man's perception of himself, but also that is *may* be an imprint in nature. If there is such an imprint, then science and mathematics also may develop new and productive insights into their particular disciplines.

BIBLIOGRAPHY

Badcock, C.R. *The Psychoanalysis of Culture*. Oxford: Basil Blackwell, 1980.

Barnes, Harry E. "The Social and Political Philosophy of Auguste Comte: Positivist Utopia and the Religion of Humanity." *An Introduction to the History of Sociology*. Harry E. Barnes (Ed.). Chicago: University of Chicago Press, 1948.

Barnes, Harry E. "William Graham Sumner: Spencerianism in American Dress." *An Introduction to the History of Sociology*. Harry E. Barnes (Ed.). Chicago: University of Chicago Press, 1949.

Benoit-Smullyan, Emile. "The Sociologism of Emile Durkheim and His School." *An Introduction to the History of Sociology*. Harry E. Barnes (Ed.). Chicago: University of Chicago Press, 1948.

Bidney, David. *Theoretical Anthropology*. New York: Columbia University Press, 1953.

Bigongiari, Dino. *The Political Ideas of St. Thomas Aquinas*. New York: Hafner, 1969.

Boaz, Franz. *Race, Language and Culture*. New York: The Free Press, 1940.

Bohannan, Paul. "Conscience Collective and Culture." *Emile Durkheim 1858-1917*. Kurt H. Wolff (Ed.). New York: Arno Press, 1979.

Bourguignon, Erika. *Psychological Anthropology: An Introduction to Human Nature and Cultural Differences*. New York: Holt, Rinehart and Winston, 1971.

Breger, Louis. *Freud: Darkness in the Midst of Vision*. New York: John Wiley & Sons, 2000.

Brown, Donald. *Human Universals*. Philadelphia: Temple University Press, 1991.

Caputo, Michael. *God Seen Through the Eyes of the Greatest Minds*. West Monroe, LA: Howard Publishing, 2000.

Claessen, Henri J.M. and Pieter van de Velde. "The Evolution of Sociopolitical Organizations." *Development and Decline: The Evolution of Sociopolitical Organization*. Henri J.M. Claessen, Pieter van de Velde and M Estellie Smith (Eds.). South Hadley, MA: Bergin & Garvey Publishers, 1985.

Comte, Auguste. *A General View of Positivism*. New York: Robert Speller & Sons, 1957.

Cornford, Francis M. *The Republic of Plato*. London: Oxford University Press, 1970.

Cranston, Maurice. (Ed.) *Locke on Politics, Religion, and Education*. New York: Collier Books, 1965.

Dalton, George. "Aboriginal Economies in Stateless Societies." *Exchange Systems in Prehistory*. Timothy K. Earle and Jonathon E. Ericson (Eds). New York: Academic Press, 1977.

DeLaszlo, Violet. (Ed.). *The Basic Writings of C.G. Jung*. New York: The Modern Library, 1959.

Dundes, Alan. "The Number Three in American Culture." *Every Man His Way: Readings in American Cultural Anthropology*. Alan Dundes (Ed.) Englewood Cliffs, NJ: Prentice Hall, 1966.

Durkheim, Emile. *Suicide: A Study in Sociology*. George Simpson (Ed.). New York: Free Press, 1951.

Freud, Sigmund. *The Interpretation of Dreams*. New York: Avon Books, 1968.

Freud, Sigmund. "Selection From: An Outline of Psychoanalysis. The Psychical Apparatus." *Readings for an Introduction to Psychology*. Richard A. King (Ed.). New York: McGraw-Hill, 1971.

Goldsmith, Seth. "The Status of Health Indicators," *Health Services Reports*, 87:3 (March 1972):212-220.

Greer, Ann. "The Measurement of Health in Urban Communities," *Journal of Urban Affairs*, 8 (Spring 1986): 9-21.

Hamilton, Alexander, John Jay and James Madison. *The Federalist*. New York: Modern Library, 1787.

Holmes, Lowell D. *Anthropology: An Introduction*. New York: Ronald Press, 1971.

Hothersall, David. *History of Psychology*. Philadelphia: Temple University Press, 1984.

http://bized.ac.uk/virtual/economy/library/economists/keynesth/htm.

Hume, David. *A Treatise of Human Nature*. Baltimore: Penguin, 1969.

Jones, Tom B. *Ancient Civilzation*. Chicago: Rand McNally & Co., 1960.

Keynes, John Maynard. *The General Theory of Employment, Interest, and Money*. New York: Harcourt Brace Jovanovich, Publishers, 1953.

Koenig, Samuel. Sociology: *An Introduction to the Science of Society*. New York: Barnes & Noble, 1972.

Kroeber, A. L. *Anthropology*. New York: Harcourt, Brace and Co., 1948.

Kuper, Adam. *The Chosen Primate: Human Nature and Cultural Diversity*. Cambridge: Harvard University Press, 1994.

Larson, James S. *The Measurement of Health: Concepts and Indicators*. New York: Greenwood Press, 1991.

Leaf, Murray F. *Man, Mind, and Science: A History of Anthropology*. New York: Columbia University Press, 1979.

Locke, John. *Second Treatise of Civil Government*. Chicago: Gateway, 1955.

Loustaunau, Martha O. *The Cultural Concept of Health, Illness, and Medicine*. Westport, CT: Bergin & Garvey, 1997.

Lowry, Ritchie P. *Sociology: The Science of Society*. New York: Scribner, 1969.

McDowell, Ian and Claire Newell. *Measuring Health: A Guide to Rating Scales and Questionnaires*. New York: Oxford University Press, 1987.

McGee, R. Jon and Richard Warms. *Anthropological Theory: An Introductory History*. Mountain View, CA: Mayfield Publishing Co., 1996.

McKeon, Richard. (Ed.). *Introduction to Aristotle*. New York: The Modern Library, 1947.

Morgan, Clifford T. and Richard A. King. *Introduction to Psychology*. New York: McGraw-Hill, 1966.

Murdock, George. *Theories of Illness: A World Survey*. Pittsburgh: University of Pittsburgh Press, 1980.

New American Standard Bible. Nashville: Holman Bible Publishers, 1977.

Neyer, Joseph. "Individualism and Socialism in Durkheim." *Emile Durkheim 1858-1917*. Kurt H. Wolff (Ed.). New York: Arno Press, 1979.

Ricardo, David. "Principles of Economy and Taxation" (1817). *Masterworks of Economics*. Leonard Abbott (Ed.). Garden City, NY: Doubleday, 1946.

Ritzer, Gorge. *Sociological Theory*. New York: Alfred A. Knopf, 1983.

Salomon, Albert. "The Legacy of Durkheim." *Emile Durkheim 1858-1917*. Kurt H. Wolff (Ed.). New York: Arno Press, 1979.

Samson, Colin. (Ed.). *Health Studies: A Critical and Cross-Cultural Reader*. Oxford: Blackwell Publishers, 1999.

Samuelson, Paul and William Nordhaus *Economics, 16th Edition*. Boston: McGraw Hill, 1998.

Service, Elman R. *Origins of the State and Civilization: The Process of Cultural Evolution*. New York: Norton, 1975.

Simons-Morton, Bruce, Walter Greene and Nell Gottlieb. *Introduction to Health Education and Promotion, 2nd Edition*. Prospect Heights, IL: Waveland Press, 1995.

Skinner, B.F. *Science and Human Behavior*. New York: The Free Press, 1965.

Smelser, Neil J. *Sociology*. Cambridge, MA: Blackwell, 1994.

Smith, Adam. *The Wealth of Nations*. New York: Modern Library, 1937.

Smith, Adam, "From Adam Smith." *Man & The State: The Political Philosophers*. Saxe Commins and Robert Linscott (Eds.). New York: Washington Square Press, 1966.

Solomon, Paul. "The Triune Concept." *Body, Mind & Spirit: The Journey Toward Health and Wholeness*. Peter Albright and Bets Albright (Eds.) Brattleboro, VT: Greene Press, 1980.

Soule, George. *Ideas of the Great Economists*. New York: Mentor Books, 1952.

Stagner, Ross. *A History of Psychological Theories*. New York: Collier MacMillan, 1988.

Sumner, William G. *War and Other Essays*. Albert G. Keller (Ed.). New York: Ams Press, 1970.

Tanakh: *A New Translation of the Holy Scriptures According to the Original Hebrew Text*. Philadelphia: The Jewish Publication Society, 1985.

Taylor, Henry O. *Ancient Ideals, Volume II, 2nd Ed.* New York: MacMillan Co., 1930.

The American Heritage Dictionary, Second College Edition. Boston: Houghton Mifflin, 1985.

Thompson, Kenneth. Auguste Comte: *The Foundation of Sociology*. New York: John Wiley & Sons, 1975.

Tobin, James. "An Overview of the General Theory." *A 'Second Edition' of the General Theory*. G.C. Harcourt and P.A. Riach (Eds.). London: Routledge, 1997.

Tylor, Sir Edward Burnett. *Researches into the Early History of Mankind and the Development of Civilization*. Chicago: University of Chicago Press, 1964.

Unger, Merrill F. *Unger's Bible Dictionary*. Chicago: Moody Press, 1966.

Watson, John B. *Behaviorism*. New York: WW Norton, 1970.

Weber, Max. *The Protestant Ethic and the Spirit of Capitalism*. New York: Charles Scribner's Sons, 1958.

Willard, Dallas. "Gray matter and the soul," *Christianity Today*, 46:12.

WWW_groups.dcs.st-and.ac.uk/~history/mathematicians/keynes.html.

WWW.threes.com

y Salmoran, Rolando Tamyo. "The Judicial Litigation in Early Stages and the Evolution of the Legal Process." *Development and Decline: The Evolution of*

Sociopolitical Organization. Henri J.M. Claessen, Pieter van de Velde and M Estellie Smith (Eds.). South Hadley, MA: Bergin & Garvey Publishers, 1985.

INDEX

F

G

H

I

J

K

L

M

N

P